FROM ONE EXTREME
TO ANOTHER

THE STORY OF
MINISTER MICHAEL GORDON

(aka Colonel, Big Youth, Chabba, and Brother Michael)

TAMARE
HOUSE

From One Extreme to Another

The Story
of
Minister Michael Gordon

Published in Great Britain with TamaRe House Publishers
January 2013
25 Brixton Station Road, London, SW9 8PB, United Kingdom
info@tamarehouse.com
www.tamarehouse.co.uk
044 (8)44 357 2592

This publication employs archival-quality paper.

A CIP record of this publication is available from the British Library

ISBN: 978-1-908552-27-3

Cover design and layout by
Third-i-Design

Editorial Services by Kwemara Publications

Contents

Acknowledgements

I give thanks to God for life and for making it possible for me to achieve all good things in life, and for guiding and protecting me through the storms.

To my loving wife, **Elizabeth**, and six children God has blessed us with: **Anecia**, **Kemisha**, **Jason**, **Shamar**, **Romario**, and **Joel**; also the rest of my entire Family – with no exceptions, I love you all and may God bless and guide you all.

To the team which I was fortunate to be blessed with to assist me in the publication of my book, such as Ras Kwende, my proof-editor; my agent, Lloyd Osbourne; my marketing consultant, Michelle Grant, and the entire staff at TamaRe House publishers. May God bless and guide you all.

Anyone whom I have mentioned in this book, who in the past had done me wrong, regardless of what, I have forgiven every one of them. I have no bitterness. There are also those whom I have mentioned, who may feel offended because I have exposed the truth. But whatever I have said had to be told, so no hard feelings. And if you cannot accept it, so be it. May God bless and guide you all.

Minister Michael Gordon

NOTE: Many of the names in this story have been changed to maintain anonymity and avoid embarrassment.

Preface

Greetings, dear reader

My name is Michael Gordon (also known by many as Colonel, Big Youth, Chabba, Brother Michael, and now as Minister Gordon). This book, which is called *From One Extreme to Another*, is a true story of my life. I believe it could not have been given a more appropriate title, which I feel you too will appreciate after reading it. Every one of us has a story to tell of the experiences we face in life, within which there is a wide magnitude of joys, trials, tribulations and triumphs.

I wrote this book because I feel a great need to share with others certain circumstances I have encountered, overcome and endured, so that you will be enlightened and, if possible, motivated.

For many of you who have known me for many years, certain revelations about my life may leave you astounded when you learn of them. For those of you to whom I am a complete stranger, or just another author who has written a book, again I believe you will find areas of a deep connection when reflecting on your own life.

This book is my autobiography or memoirs but it is also much more. It starts off historically, telling what it was like living in one of London's most famous inner city areas, Brixton, during the 1960s to the early 1980s. It gives you an accurate and in-depth revelation of Black people's life at that time, which, in addition to the church, included another crucial aspect of our cultural cohesion and structure – our music. During this time, our music was transmitted almost exclusively through the greatest outlet channel for the African-Caribbean community then – the **sound system**. My story moves later on to the place where the sound system originated from, the capital of the reggae music business, Jamaica. Here again it reveals and in-depth account of life in the sound system and the music business world – not from a researcher point of view but direct from a man who has lived it to the fullness.

Although I am of Jamaican heritage, and speak the language thoroughly, I nevertheless had to adapt to the contrast of living in a totally different environment to that of my birth and upbringing. Naturally, however, certain aspects are similar in both countries with regard to the sound system world and life in general. I give you a behind the scenes account of the constant sound rivalry where you had to be on top of your game to survive. As well as appreciating the grace and beauty within individuals, I also examine the age-old but still mystifying realities of how people's behaviour can change suddenly and dramatically; the violent and ruthless streak which some possess; the employment of that common tool of evil used by the Devil, meaning drugs; and the lust and greed for fame and money.

It was back in England that I encountered certain experiences that moved me to expose some of the most appalling tactics used by the most severe teacher in this life. He does not care who you are when he strikes you with his often lethal vengeance. Yes, Mr Illness can cause you misery and turn your life upside down. Then there is the constant battle of good over evil; a spiritual warfare which many believe does not exist, or fail to see. I have had to do battle with these forces, illness and evil, and have survived through sheer determination and by the Grace of God. Only in this way could I have come through my roller coaster life of heartbreak, mental torment, loss of wealth, a life threatening and ever-present illness to make me become more appreciative of the miracles that God has manifested for me.

My story finishes with what I see as the greatest lesson and accomplishment of my life – my conversion to accept the Lord Jesus Christ as my personal saviour by becoming a Born Again Christian. Journey with me to see why I have seriously come to realize that it is only God, and He alone (who never changes) who is in total control. Without Him and His Son (our Lord and Saviour, Jesus Christ) in our lives, we are nothing.

There are those who are going to disagree with many things I have said, and that is ok, for God gives every man a free will. I did not write this book to convince anyone but it is my duty to declare what He has done for me, and what He has done for me He will do for others. I hope you enjoy reading about my life and maybe take some encouragement from any of the positive aspects herein. May it be for you a blessing in more ways than one. God Bless you all.

Minister Michael Gordon

Glossary of various terminologies

Ah: **It's, is, am, are, to, I**, as in: (Ah fi mi – **It's** mine) (Dat ah fi yu? – **Is** that yours?) ('im ah guh – He **is** going) (Mi ah guh – I **am** going) (Yu ah hear me? – **Are** you hearing me?) (Tek dis ah school - Take this **to** school), or, as in: (Ah going – **I** am going).

Blag: To convince someone by wordplay or by trickery.

Bonafide: Genuine person; sincere, bona fide, authentic.

Bredrin: Rastafari word with the same meaning as the biblical 'brethren' (plural for a 'brother' in the faith). Now it generally means a close friend or colleague. Rastafari has also created the word 'Sistrin' for females.

Clash: A sound clash is a musical competition between two or more sound systems, playing in turn to see who has the best selection of music to provide their customers ('the crowd') with the greatest delight. This works best when the standard is high and each contestant is pressed to reply to a preceding player's selection with at least an equally good selection, or preferably one which raises a greater 'crowd' response.

Criss: To look or sound great; everything's all right or great.

Dis: Disrespect; being disrespectful.

Deh/dey: 'Is', as in, "We him **deh**?" (Where is he?).

Dem: Them.

Don: A respected boss or leader, or controller of a situation. Also a gang leader or top man in an area. Don Dada is the leader of leaders. Don when used for a gang boss originates from the Italian mafia.

Dub:	Heavy drum and bass music without vocals, usually with echo and other enchanting effects including occasional vocals. Also refers to dub plate.
Dub plate:	Metallic disc of exclusive tunes before they came on general release (pre-release). Also called 'Specials' and originally known as **Wax**.
Fiesty/ Facety:	Cheeky, or out of order.
Fi:	For.
Flex:	To flex is to hang out or relax. Flex also refers to one's behaviour pattern, attitude or mannerism.
Floss:	To show off, especially with something that is, or appears to be, expensive.
Ganja:	Cannabis, marijuana, or weed.
Ghetto blaster:	A large portable stereo cassette-radio player, popular in the 1980s for their loud tone and heavy bass.
Gwaan:	Go on; word of encouragement or appreciation.
Hafi:	Have to.
High five:	A congratulatory or celebratory slapping of the palms between two or more persons.
Hood:	Afrikan-American slang for neighbourhood.
Kill a sound person:	To defeat another sound by outdoing them in a sound clash with more enjoyable music selections.
Marga/maaga:	Skinny, bony, slim.
Massive	Mass or majority of people, or crowd of supporters.
Nick/ to nick:	English slang meaning to arrest, to steal, or prison.
Patwa:	Authentic Jamaican speaking, aka broken English (spelt, 'patois' in French derived English).

Pure:	Many, lots of, only, extremely.
Rewind:	To play a tune again; to "pull up"/"haul an' pull up".
Rizla:	A brand of rolling paper used to roll up homemade cigarettes, or spliffs.
Slam:	Sex, sexual intercourse.
Skin teeth	Joke, have a laugh. Not to skin teeth is to be serious.
Soundman:	An individual, or even several crew members of a sound system. The resistance to describe people as 'men'/'women' is influenced by the Rastafari view that 'men', whether individual or several, is or are polluted, while 'man' is, and are, the righteous original. So, an evil individual is 'a men', while 'man and man' or 'the man dem (them)' are several man.
Specials:	See 'Dub plates'.
Spliff:	A ganja or marijuana cigarette.
Tune:	A piece of recorded music; a record.
Take set	Harass, hassle, pester, annoy, and tease.
Trainers:	UK English for training shoes or sneakers.
Wanga Gut:	Greedy person.
Weed:	See Ganja.
Work:	Contraband, smuggled to be sold for profit.
Waa'pen?/ What happen?/ Wha gwaan?:	What's up? How you doing? What's happening?
Yard/yaad:	One's house or home. Also refers to Jamaica when used by a Jamaican.
Youth:	A young man.

Chapter 1

TRUE BRIXTONIAN

God is truly great that by His grace and mercy I am still here today and am able to share my life story with you. I was born in the year 1958, the 15th of November, at Lambeth Hospital near to the site of the Imperial War Museum, Kennington, shortly after my parents came to England from Jamaica. Lambeth Hospital is no longer there. When my Mother brought me home from the hospital, my first home for the first two years of my life was at Vining Street, which is off **Atlantic Road**, just before the once famous pub called **The Atlantic**, now called **The Dogstar**.

In 1965, along that same little stretch of road around the corner from Vining Street, at 54-58 Atlantic Road, there was a store called David Greig. This was a grocery store with a butcher's section, which was the equivalent of today's major stores like Tesco, but on a smaller basis. Their logo is still in the brickwork to this very day, although the building is now a modern day bistro (a small informal bar-restaurant). Go and take a look if you are curious – you will see the initials DG with a thistle in the brown tiles outside the front.

My Mother told me when I got older that I was often ill and needed a lot of TLC.[1] She often wondered at times if I would make it through those difficult periods.

In 1960, from the age of two-plus, we moved to where my story began in earnest – the famous **Somerleyton Road.** This road has its place in history in more ways than one. I can remember hearing stories about a

---

[1] TLC – tender loving care

certain female member of the Royal Family visiting Somerleyton Road to seek her sexual pleasure with certain individuals in the local community. It was from this road that I began the start of an action-packed life which included the teachings of ghetto life in **Brixton.** I do not regret one moment of this life for it was there I learnt how to adapt to any situation that I was to find myself in until this very day.

There are those who say they know Brixton but do they really know it in-depth like I and other true Brixtonians do? I was always very forward for my age so the memories I recall from the tender age of five are those of a very perceptive child being brought up in one of London's most prolific areas – Brixton.

 The mass of my recollections begin with me as a five year old child from the year 1963. As a child in those days, if you had six pence in your pocket the amount of sweets you could buy could have fed an army. The currency then was pounds, shillings, and pence, before decimalisation came in. Most of the sweets we bought then were the unwrapped boiled sweets which were weighed out in ounces and sold from big glass jars. There were classics like Pineapple Chunks (aka Pineapple Cubes), Cola Cubes, Sherbet Lemons, and Aniseed Twists. There were also pre-wrapped sweets as well, such as Fruit Salads, Black Jack chews, and Bazooka bubble gum, but not forgetting the bags of crisps[2] containing a small wrapper with salt (to "salt 'n' shake"), which has now surfaced again. A popular chocolate bar was Bar Six, similar to today's Kit-Kat, but sectioned cross-bar, instead.

The top cars of that time were the Morris Oxford, Ford Zephyr, Austin Cambridge, Wolseley, and the infamous Bubble car which, today, would look so comical it would attract much laughter.

In those days Somerleyton Road was lined on both sides with three-storey Victorian basement houses – nothing like now. They had back

---

[2] Mostly called 'chips' elsewhere.

gardens with walls so low you could easily jump over them. These gardens went the complete length of the road and ran parallel with the train line nearby. Very few back yards, however, had any flowers in them; most grew wild with stinging nettles.

The houses were owned by private landlords who maximised usage of the ample spaces by renting out individual rooms, so oftentimes there could be up to four different families plus single occupants in the same dwelling. It was not uncommon for one to get along with some of their co-dwellers, but not with others, leading to arguments.

Most of the children I knew had to attend Sunday school, as I did, for knowing about the Lord was of prior importance to the majority of Caribbean (so-called West Indian) parents even though some may not have attended church regularly. The vehicle which would pick us up from our homes and ferry us to church was a Thames van with finger tip gear change and an engine which was inside the body of the vehicle. Lace curtains were often put up at the windows for a degree of privacy.

Even though I did not grow up with my Father I can remember him buying one of these Thames vans when he learned to drive and he would transport his fellow workers to their workplace over in Kingston-upon-Thames. For a weekly fee he would pick them up at Brixton Town Hall in Acre Lane at 5.30am every morning. My Local church was one at Brixton Hill where I attended Sunday school and services regularly, so it is no surprise that over forty five years later I have become a Born Again Christian, giving my life to the Lord.

Later on in the mid 60s, the local council purchased a lot of the houses on the street and refurbished them into three or four-roomed apartments at an affordable rental cost, which allowed families to have a separate front room. For those who did not already have one, it was the perfect opportunity to purchase the famous **Blue Spot gram** so that Mum and Dad could play those unforgettable Jim Reeves and **ska** and blue beat records. Blue Spot (Blaupunkt) grams were German-made gramophone record players much favoured by Caribbean people for their heavy bass tone.

Back then, front rooms in Caribbean homes did not have the significance their other names (living rooms or sitting rooms) would suggest. Typically, we were only allowed in the front room when visitors came and Mum wanted to show off the cabinet full of special crockery, as well as those ghastly photos which, it seemed, every Caribbean family took at **Harry Jacob** photographic studio with the same boring backdrop. This studio, which was on Landor Road in Stockwell, served a useful purpose since owning your own camera in those days was not a common occurrence.

Many people like my Mother had migrated from the Caribbean (the West Indies) in the late 40s through to the 60s to seek a better life in Britain but were in for a reality shock on finding out that all that glittered was not gold in the so-called 'mother country' of the empire. So one of the ways they dealt with the rejection which they faced was to build their own little empire in a close-knit community. I can remember at the end of Somerleyton Road, nearer to Coldharbour Lane, was where you would find a few gambling houses, obviously illegal but nevertheless in operation. These gambling places were mainly in the basement of the houses but the men would gather and socialise on the pavement along the street, especially in the summertime. This was the start of the original "Frontline" before it became known at the location on Railton Road.

Brixton Market has not known a lot of changes over the years and a few of the old traders are still about. It was originally a place where slaves were sold way before my time. My recollection of it was my having to follow my Mother to do the family shopping. At that time bacon was six pence for a pound in weight. I remember once, after leaving the butchers, asking my Mum if I could have a toy car. She replied, "Boy, you better go look for work, 'bout you want car." Apart from having to wait around for Mum to finish her discussion with friends she would run into, I generally enjoyed my trips to Brixton Market.

The big chemists of those days are generally now called pharmacies. The one known as **Timothy Whites** was situated on the same spot where **Boots** is today, with a smaller branch on Atlantic Road. Across the road from Timothy Whites was Colliers, selling electrical appliances, furnishings and other household items on **Electric Avenue** (one of the first roads to have electric light). Let us not forget **Woolworths** on Brixton Road, which closed down in 2009 due to the financial crisis known as the credit crunch. **Morley's** department store was over on the other side, along with **Bon Marche**. Further along were an up-class store and a big clothing department store called **C&A**, which no longer exists.

Mum had to make sure that certain favourites were on the shopping list. I would be the most miserable child if she did not buy my favourite cereal – none other than Kellogg's Rice Crispies, which I had to have, served with hot milk, the last thing before I went to bed. Two other popular cereals from those days were Sugar Puffs and Cornflakes. The white sliced breads preferred by Caribbean people were Nevilles, Mother's Pride and good old Sunblest.

Most Jamaican parents did not do major cooking on Fridays. It was the lovely fry-up of eggs, sausage, bacon and beans and a big bowl of cornmeal or hominy-corn porridge, or oats porridge, rotated with the great British dish – you guessed it, Fish and Chips from your local chip shop. Ours was across the road from my primary school in Effra Road.

Saturday's menu never changed, though. That was always soup day – beef soup, red peas soup or chicken soup, all cooked with dumplings, yam and carrots. I hated them but when I got older, I loved my soup. Sunday's menu provided the best meal of the week – Rice and Peas (red kidney beans) and Chicken, which is still a firm favourite with Jamaicans (and some other Caribbeans) to this day. Beetroot juice or carrot juice or Guinness punch was your drink. If as a child your taste buds could not handle those, there was diluted syrup or a brand of orange squash called Tree Top which, when mixed together with the Jamaican Syrup, was lovely. My Mother always made sure our bellies were filled.

Cigarettes popular among people who smoked then were brands without filter tips, like **Woodbine**, **Park Drive**, **Senior Service** and the dreaded **Capstan** full strength which my uncle used to smoke. There were also the filtered brands like **Player's No. 6** and **Consulate**, the only menthol option in that period.

Oh, how times have changed the meaning of words. For example, the word **gay** meant you were happy and had nothing to do with your sexual preference. Again, a condom was called a **Johnny bag** and was sold in small brown envelopes taken from under the counter by the sales person in the chemist/pharmacy.

Can you, if you were about in those times, remember the first set of Indian migrants that came over and became the door to door salesmen selling Candlewick bed spreads? The one that used to visit Somerleyton Road was called **Baboo.** His catch phrase was, "Very good quality, you take now and pay me weekly."

Further on down the years they took over the traditional post offices. When the English post masters were in control, they only sold stamps, postal orders (money orders), and postal transactions. However, when the Indian businessmen took over the post offices, they sold a wide range of goods, also.

There was a somewhat unscrupulous insurance company who played on the ignorance of mainly Black people, selling them worthless life policies and saving schemes. They were called **United Friendly** and their agents would come round once a fortnight and collect contribution premiums. It was only when the policies came to maturity many years later that our parents found out they were worth very little and far below their expectations. The name of the agent that used to collect my Mum's money was Jimmy, a white English man. I can still see his face now in my memories, sweet talking and appearing to fancy all of his Caribbean (so-called West Indian) women clients.

The emergence of street gangs among the white working class male youngsters was in force during those times. Following on from the Teddy Boys of the previous decade, in the early sixties you had the **Mods** and the **Rockers** (aka Greasers) and then the shaven headed **Skinheads** of the late 60s, all with their particular mode of dressing and all of whom did not take a liking to the growing ethnic minority in their country. The Mods used to wear long parker coats and ride Lambretta and Vesper motor scooters with long whip aerials on the back. Their rivals, the Rockers rode the heavier motor bikes like the northern Triumphs. The original skinheads of the 60s (unlike their later adaptation) were influenced by the music and fashion of the earlier Mods and the Jamaican settlers. All these gangs were ever ready for confrontation, even against each other, so what chance did the Black youths stand? But I tell you what; they held their ground on many occasions, to the surprise of everyone.

The Black youngsters always liked to dress immaculately, following in the footsteps of their parents, so suits were preferred, especially when going out. There were some classy dressers in those days, among both men and women. Fashionable men would wear suits with seams that seemed sharp to cut, made from the classic pinstripe cloth and later on from the two-tone tonic material (a shiny mohair-type fabric that changes colour in different light and angles). These suits were made by immigrant tailors who came to Britain with tailoring as a profession. Later on in the mid 70s, local tailor shops such as Derek Munn on Station Road, near the recreation centre, would start getting the trade.

Two of the slickest dressers in those times were characters called Hiker and Frankie. I can remember as a little boy saying, "Man, I want to dress like them when I get older." The immaculate look also included tidy looking hair. Girls wore neatly plaited or straightened hair and the dads, the young men, and boys regularly visited the barber shop, which was at first in some of our Mums' or dads' friends houses, before some of them were lucky enough to acquire shop premises.

The barber shop was where you heard conversation about every topic there was. The favourite for discussion was boxing and the favourite boxer was none other than the great Cassius Clay, later to be known as Muhammad Ali. Cricket came next, followed by politics. While the barber is engaging in these debates, you would have to sit quietly until he was ready to resume cutting your hair and, as a child, you had no say whatsoever about what style you had. Your hair would be completely cut off and that was it. The clippers or shares they used then were not electric; they were the dreaded manual mechanical type which gave you untold pulls and pinches. Those who do not know these clippers should be thankful.

One of the well known barbers of that time was Larkie. His shop was situated directly in front of Brixton market arcade on Coldharbour Lane. The other one was Dave's at Leeson Road just off Mayall Road.

This was the one my Mother would take me to, and where I continued going by myself when I got older.

I lived at 82 Somerleyton Road and at 86 was a basement drinking den called the Spring Vale. This was run by Mr. Buck, who installed a juke box in place for entertainment and boarded up the windows with a little sign outside.

The next major road running parallel with Somerleyton Road was Geneva Road, which no longer exists as it was buried beneath the Moorlands Estate development of the 1970s. Back then you could gain access via Geneva Terrace which was across from my house at the end of Somerleyton. Going the other way it ran into Loughborough Park where I was to live in the 70s. There was also and still is the Guinness Trust block of flats where in those days only white English families were allowed to live. Nowadays, however, it is occupied by people of various origins.

Many of my friends either lived on Somerleyton Road or Geneva Road. There was the Harris family, the Marshalls, and the Wilsons – all well known as large families. I also know what hardship is like, being single-handedly brought up with my three other siblings by my Mother.

My Mother had three jobs to try and make ends meet. Even though things may have been cheaper in those times, so were the wages. When I look back on the sacrifices she had to make she deserved the biggest accolade.

Chapter 2

PARAFFIN HEATER DAYS

Many houses in those days did not have the luxury of a bathroom or an inside toilet. You would have to bath in one of those tin wash pans or use the public baths. The nearest one to us was Clapham Manor Bath house on Clapham Manor Street. Where the toilet was concerned this was outside at the back of the house. Can you imagine having to use these late at night in winter time? It was like a living nightmare because the British winter in the 1960s and 70s were much colder than they are today.

There was no central heating, either; it was the good old coal fire (mainly in the front room) or mostly paraffin (kerosene) heaters. There were two types – the one that burned the paraffin from a circular wick, and the other where the paraffin was burnt on a metal mesh dome. Paraffin heaters caused lots of water to condense on windows and walls, leading to dampness. Add to this the dangerous burnt paraffin fumes and carbon monoxide produced in badly ventilated rooms, as well as the danger of the heaters being knocked over, and it is easy to see why many people experienced "sooty noses" and suffered from bronchitis, coughs, headaches, and some fatal accidents. Some residents even cooked on paraffin stoves because some privately rented house had not yet been installed with gas cookers. The paraffin truck would come round twice a week. The two main suppliers were Oily Oily, a White man who wore glasses, and Sapper, who was a Black man. Half a crown or 2/6 (two and six, or two shillings and six pence) was the price of a gallon.

INNER LONDON EDUCATION AUTHORITY

EFFRA PRIMARY SCHOOL

REPORT FOR YEAR ENDING JULY, 1969.

Name.... MICHAEL GORDON

Number in Class.... 40

Class.... 3.M

Position in Class....

SUBJECT		ASSESSMENT	REMARKS
ENGLISH	Reading		Michael can read well and
	Spelling		takes a good interest in books
	Written		His written work is neat and
	Composition		of quite a good standard.
ARITHMETIC	Mental / Written		His creative writing is most
HISTORY			imaginative.
GEOGRAPHY			Michael has tackled his new
SCIENCE			number work well.
ART			
WRITING			Changed from printing to writing
HANDWORK	Needlework		
OTHER SUBJECTS	Physical Education		Member of the school football
	Music		team

Religious Knowledge.... Satisfactory

Attendance.... Good.

GENERAL REPORT

Michael is a very friendly, helpful boy. He tends to be rather excitable but is most popular. He is capable of good work.

.... S. A. Macdonald.... ~~Class Master~~
Class Mistress

A. A. ...... Head Master
~~Head Mistress~~

My Primary School Report, 1969

In 1963 I started my primary education at Effra Primary School. One entrance was situated in Barnwell Road, the other in Effra Parade. There were other primary schools in the area but none more famous than Effra – it was the place to be. The headmistress of the infant school was a Miss Rosa Lampard and although she was quite elderly,

23

none of the pupils could outrun her so it was no use trying to escape if she made after you. The headmaster for the juniors was Mr. Nicholson, a strict disciplinarian who took no prisoners and would not hesitate to introduce you to the cane (a thin long stick used to hit you with). You may be surprised to find out that many other pupils who became well known in Brixton over the years turned out to have also attended Effra.

From that age of four-plus I always liked to follow the big boys – mainly my elder brother, Delroy, who was a popular character in the area. He was always up to mischief, which caused our Mother a lot of grief. I would always be running behind his tail and because I learnt a lot from him I was more street wise than all of my peers. I was exposed to the adult way of thinking from this early age, which stood me in good stead.

The comics books that we used to read and were popular back then were **The Beano**, with characters like **Dennis the Menace**; **The Dandy**, with **Desperate Dan** who had a huge appetite for eating cow pies; the **DC Comics** with the super heroes, **Batman** and **Superman;** and the **Marvel Comics** with **Captain Marvel, Spiderman and the Fantastic Four**, to name a few.

When we did get a black and white television, my favourite programmes were **Lassie; Flipper** (the Dolphin); ITV's **Ready Steady Go!**, which was before the BBC's Top of the Pops; **The Beverley Hillbillies** with main character **Jed Clampet**; the **Invisible Man**; **The Saint,** whose character was **Simon Templar,** played by **Roger Moore;** and the soap opera, **Crossroads,** which was my Mother's favourite.

All the older boys and girls in the area went to the local youth club in Railton Road, called **Shepherd's** after the name of the youth leader, Gavton Shepherd, who was running it at that time. Although it was the older children who attended, I was not going to be left out so I attended also. The youth club building is still standing today within the local Railton Road Methodist Church hall. It is now called Railton Methodist Youth & Community Centre, although many still refer to it as Shepherd's.

Back then, as a younger child attending a club for older youth, older ones looked after me because I showed them respect and they loved my mature attitude, which sometimes led me into all kinds of mischief. Because of my association with older children, I had, from an early age, an understanding of the intimate side of a relationship between men and women. My favourite game was playing mother and father (also called dolly house) and obviously I was the father while the daughter of one of the other tenants would be the mother. I played this role of the father fully, no holds barred; all I had to do was to make sure we were never caught doing what I should not have been doing at that age, albeit my maturity was way beyond my age. This got to a stage where I was engaging fully with girls my age and older whenever the occasion would arise. I was imitating what I was exposed to by my older peers.

My true love at the time was for music, and **sound system** was in me from the age of 8 years old. This love of music was further fuelled by my Mother's love for dancing, for she would take me to dances with her from an early age (from the age of 9). The major social/cultural outlets for Black people at that time were the church and our popular music. Back then, our music was transmitted publicly through the greatest outlet channel for the African-Caribbean community then – the **sound system**.

The original sound systems of the 60s were **Sir Coxsone, Duke Reid, Duke Lee, Neville the Musical Enchanter, Soferno-B, Jim Daddy, Count Shelly, Duke Vin, Count Suckle, Sir Ivano, Young's Impression,** and **Lord Koos.**

Later on emerged **Lord Gellys, V-Rocket, The Untochables, Sebastian The High Priest,** and **D-Nunes,** who was originally a North London sound who come over and started playing in South London. The first time I listened to D-Nunes he was playing in a **blues dance** (Jamaican house party or shub-in[3]) at Loughborough Park, Brixton. They had a very good selector[4] by the name Clivey and one of D-Nunes' signature tune was *Investigator* by Cornell Campbell. Their resident venue was at Gartree Road in New Cross but they had the regular blues crowd from Brixton for a long time before Soferno-B took control of that crowd. Apart from Soferno, who I used to play with as part of his crew, I personally listened to all of these sounds, plus some which I have not mentioned and some others that I have forgotten. There was also the **7/11Go-Go Club** which was a regular dance venue for D-Nunes, Soferno-B, Sir Coxsone, and Duke Reid in those days. It was housed in a large Victorian house in Vauxhall, right on the one way system on Kennington Road and was owned by a man named Banjee. Those were the days.

The year now was 1967. I was 9 years old and was always finding things of interest to do so I asked my Mum if I could join the Cub Scouts. The group I joined was the one that used our school hall for meetings. They were the 12th South Lambeth and the leader was George Kenwood. When I got older I went into the Boy Scouts but this still was not enough for me.

My Mother at that time could best be described as the original "dance hall queen". She was a top class dancer and when she took to the dance floor, all other ladies would have to vacate it. Any male dance partner had to be above average to partner her or they would be

---

[3] 'Shub-in' is the Jamaican pronunciation of the Irish word, 'sibin' (shebeen) – a club or bar where liquor is sold without licence.

[4] The success of a sound system depends to a large degree on the skill of the selector of the music played on that sound. A good selector knows not only what good music to play to please his audience, but also in what order to select and play them.

quickly exposed as a novice. This was the era of the musical genres, known as the Swing, the Blues, Ska, and Bluebeat. The popular artistes of those days included Fats Domino and Don Drummond and the Skatalites, to whose music the men would do the shuffle – a very energetic solo dance and a sight to behold.

For a nine year old to have full experience of all this was very uncommon. I would be listening to great sounds like Sir Coxsone, Duke Reid, Count Shelly, Duke Lee, Neville the Musical Enchanter and the great Soferno-B, for whom I would later on be his main selector.

The first open air dance I experienced was a one-off event kept at the top of Somerleyton Road in 1968 on a plot of land, later to be used as an adventure playground. What excitement it was to see and hear the great Duke Reid the Trojan, and Sir Coxsone doing musical battle with their massive, heavy-sound generating valve amplifiers and the contrasting top-end and mid-range steel horns. Today's equivalent would be the transistorised amplifier and the tweeter. The exclusive tunes which were played then were called **wax**, later on known as Dub plates (see the glossary).

I became so in love with these vibes that I promised myself that I must become a top sound-man one day. Fortunately for me, my older brother was also a music lover who was going to the big dances and clubs and telling me what it was like. I would every so often get the chance to attend some of these dances, and even clubs.

I do not personally know anyone my age who can say they went to the popular Roaring Twenties night club on Carnaby Street in London's West End at the age of 11years old. The Roaring Twenties was run by Count Suckle, a popular deejay who had settled in the UK in the early 1950s. I went there one night with Soferno-B who was playing that night as a stand-in for Sir Coxsone, who was playing at Rochester Hall in Kent at one of the then popular coach outing dances.

The Brixton Town Hall was another popular venue for the big sounds to play and the annual Gold Cup Clash, which I attended in 1968, was a real eye opener. The three heavyweights in contention that night were **Duke Reid, Neville The Enchanter,** and **Count Shelly** from north London. At this time, Cecil, who now owns King Tubby's, was one of Duke Reid's senior men and I heard him say to other followers of Duke Reid that certain judges said that no matter what the Duke plays he would not win. Can you imagine the tension before the judges' decision was given? And so said, so it was done; even though Duke Reid played the best selection they gave the decision to Neville.

Each sound would have a section of speaker boxes on the stage and they were called "house of joy" because of their size. I can remember Duke Reid's set - it was called **Jug Head**. When the winner was announced, all hell broke loose! The section of boxes which were on the stage was pushed over, crashing several feet to the dance floor below, and weapons were being brandished. It was definitely time for me to make an exit; this was not the place for a boy of ten. These brothers took the sound business seriously but thank God nobody was killed.

There were three soundmen surnamed "Duke" in those days – Duke Reid, Duke Vin (from North London), and Duke Lee. Duke Lee's sound was not as big in relative size of equipment as some of the other sounds then, but when it came to sound quality and selection of tune you had to rate him. There was a club called **El Partido** in Peckham, and also Blue Ribbon which Duke Reid played regularly. His main selectors were Diamond (aka Greeney) and Abraham (who ended up migrating to Canada and building a sound also called Duke Reid). They were two great selectors of that time.

Stay with me to find out about soundman history from an eye-witness perspective from the days of my youth and not from research or from short-term experience. Everyone with experience will want to express it in some way but one should express oneself in proportion to their experience and have due regard for those with great experience and achievement.

As I said before, Brixton always had places for social entertainment, such as the Fridge nightclub (now closed and reopened as Electric Brixton), which was formerly the **ABC Cinema**. Every Saturday morning was the matinee programme for the ABC minors and we would go there from 10am in the morning till about 12.30pm to watch films such as comic-book heroes like Captain Marvel, Zorro, Lone Ranger, Batman, Champion the Wonder Horse, Lassie, and lots more. The other cinema, just across the road, was called the Classic, also known as "bug house", and now called the **Ritzy**.

The Brixton club that provided a variety of popular musical pleasure was called the **RamJam,** situated just across from the police station, at 390 Brixton Road above a shoe shop called **Elaine Barry**. This was a venue that Sir Coxsone would play regularly. Going to one of these reggae sessions, one had to dress the part. The aftershave used by most young men was **Brut**, and if you did not have a woollen **Crombie** coat, not forgetting your silk handkerchief in the top outside breast pocket of your suit, you were out of touch.

If you could not afford to go to the club, the main place for dancing was the popular **blues dance,** aka a **house party.** This was where the word 'limit' would go out of the window. I, at ten years old, was amazed to find that one house could hold up to two or three hundred people in two to five rooms. Sounds ridiculous, but it's true.

They would start from about 10pm Saturday night and go on till 7, 8, or 9 in the morning, or even till mid-day Sunday. Sometimes they would be raided by the police as the neighbours might complain about the noise level of the sound systems playing. The wallpaper would regularly suffer from extraordinary wear and tear after these dances. This was because the main locations in the rooms were the walls, where you could really **wine** (gyrate your waist) in maximum close-body contact with your female partner leaning on the wall for firm support.

Drinks that would be available were **Cherry B, Babycham, Long Life Beer, Teacher's Whisky, Barley Wine** (the then Golden Label brand of strong beer) and, in early 70s, the dreaded **Carlsberg Special Brew** which wrecked the lives of many men. Cooked food was also sold, such as **curry goat and rice; mackerel and green banana;** and not leaving out the **Jamaican patties**, usually home-made and full of hot pepper.

Brixton was very popular for blues dances, also nearby areas such as **Clapham, Battersea**, and **Peckham**. The roads in Brixton which regular blues dances were kept were **Mayall Road, Mostyn Road, Solan Road, Railton Road, Shakespeare Road, Hayter Road, Lambeth Road, Concanon Street** and **Saltoun Road** (commonly pronounced Soulton). The most famous road in the 70s for blues dances (better known as the regular shub-ins) was the famous **Villa Road** (in SW9) where I personally played six nights a week with **Soferno-B Sound** while I was still attending secondary school, having the occasional nights off when it got too much. When I look back and think about those times I can identify with the modern youths who (many, like myself then) have great academic potential but often channel this into to a less significant direction which, depending on the individual, can leave them with a weakened self esteem and a constant uphill struggle to get motivated and back on track. I am thankful I was able to dig deep and turned the negative into positive, which was hard to do when you got caught up in the sweetness which we were led to believe was the great street life.

The late great **Nyah Ochi** was in charge at the time but he has now passed on. R.I.P, original Rude Boy from the 60s. I learnt a lot from him. No one stepped out of line with him in those days or you knew what to expect. The same situation applies today; it is just a different set of players. There has always been postcode (area) warfare but back then it would be described as territorial control. Brixton men always saw themselves as the trend setters in all areas of life, from fashion to street credibility, and they were always regarded with caution, even awe, by others. What has happened now is that the table has turned and the hardcore youths now give no special regard to whether one comes from Brixton or Yard (Jamaica). The same youth who would say, as an initial greeting, "What's gwaanin fam?" will just as readily say: "I don't care, I will do a boy something," if they feel they might be wronged, harmed or even disrespected. The Jamaican hardcore would say, "We have di place lock." Quite often temptation would creep into my thoughts to follow the hardcore element, especially mixing with them left, right, and centre. But I restrained from doing so and eventually I saw the benefits from not making the wrong decision. It is so easy to get caught up in a moment of madness which will often leave you with a lifetime of regret.

The young blues dance lovers would walk to and from several house parties to listen to their favourite sounds play, hence the name **Trodders** was given to them by the few privileged ones who may have owned a **Ford Cortina,** a **Ford Anglia,** or a **Mini Cooper.** The less fortunate could not afford to run a car or take a taxi – and anyway, a black cab driver would not pick up a Black man, especially late at night, so it was 'ankle express' (reaching your destination by walking) for many.

I experienced a lot of blues dances even before I became a fully fledged selector from as early as 1968. Consequently, I have seen some things that would make you cringe with fear, but I loved every minute of it. The Black community of Brixton has never had a great relationship with the Police from way back in the 60s. Racism was rife and they would drive around the neighbourhoods in prisoner-transport vans called Black Marias, which was intimidating to many Black youths, so anything was liable to happen. All their drinks would be confiscated and on occasions, after the waving of batons and some youth being planted with 'illegal substances' (drugs), several arrests would be made. This was the regular practice of certain officers. I even witnessed them loading a complete sound system into the back of their van on a couple of occasions.

The site that Foot Locker sports shop now occupies was originally **Burtons Menswear** shop, and round the corner on Brixton Road was **Dunn & Co**, selling all the felt hats, ties, and English gents suits which were not meant for the lads of Somerleyton Road.

The 60s had been a real eye opener in preparing me for what was to emerge in the 70s. I was about to leave primary education and move unto secondary school in September 1969. Some of my close friends would be going to the same secondary school which I had gotten into while the others would be attending elsewhere. I would now be in completely different surroundings with new challenges to face.

The secondary school which I had gotten into was called **Beaufoy**, in Lollard Street, Kennington, right next to the famous **Lambeth Walk**, home to one of the all time great comedians, **Charlie Chaplin**. At that stage I was 11 years old but had the life experience of a 21-year old, which made me stand out above the rest. My nickname at that time was the **Colonel**, which was given to me during my boy-scout days. We had visited an army barracks and the colonel placed his hat on my head, saying he could see leadership in me and everyone started calling me the Colonel, which was to be my alias for a few years.

BEAUFOY SCHOOL (comprehensive)

Lollard Street, London SE11 6PY

REPORT for period from ....SEPT 73.... to ....JULY 74....

on (names in full) ....GORDON MICHAEL....

House ....WREN.... Tutor Group ....8.... Form ....45.

Subject	Set	Mark % AUT SER SUM			Comment	
English		A2	A2	A2	A good, hard working boy	G.S.
Religious Education						
Geography						
Geology						
History		A²	A²	A²	An excellent worker	J.B.
Economics						
Commerce						
Languages						
Mathematics	½	B2	B2	B2	Steady work - Satisfactory	A.B.
Science PHYSICS				C2	Could do better	J.F.
Technical Drawing		B2	B2	B2	A very willing worker	H.F.L.
Engineering Metalwork		B2	B2	B2	He has made good progress	H.F.F
Woodwork		A2	A2	A2	Has worked very hard all year	C.G.G.
Art						
Music						
P.E. and Games		A₁	A₁		Very good	O.P.

Late ....10.... times.   Absent ....5.... times.

Michael continues to be a first-class member of the group - he possesses a cheerful disposition and is very co-operative. His mature attitude and competent leadership sets a good example to the rest of the group. He has done a good year's work and his standard of attainment is steadily improving.

Michael is a most helpful, friendly, responsible young man, popular with boys & staff alike. His House service as prefect has been invaluable. His consistent work will stand him in good stead.

Well done, Michael! — Thank you!

G R Stimpson .... Tutor Group Master

.... Housemaster

.... Headmaster

E. Gordon .... Parent's Signature

My secondary school report from Beaufoy School (now called Lilian Baylis Technology School)

33

It was not long before I became a popular person among both my age group and older pupils because when it came to knowing about street life and adult issues, the Colonel was your man. After the weekend my peers could only speak about riding their bikes or playing "knock down ginger", which was an annoying game whereby a group of them would repeatedly ring residents' doorbells or knock on their doors and then run off before they could answer. My line of discussion, on the other hand, was about what had taken place at a big dance or a house party, the record selections that were played, and often reporting on the love-hate relationships of the deejays with the female dance fans.

I was at such a crucial stage of my life; all this adult exposure and mentality which I had, surely needed to be handled with extreme care for this was where I could have gone completely off the rails and become an addition to the statistics of juvenile delinquency. My brain was always doing overtime, thinking about the adult way of life and often forgetting that I was just a little boy and not even a teenager as yet. I just wanted to be out there doing certain things adults would do.

I had in-depth knowledge of how pimps operated; their living off immoral earnings and abusing their women to the most degrading degree. Even at that young age I despised and hated the guys that plied that way of life. I always said to myself that if a man did this to my sisters, even at my age, I would find some way of taking him out, and I don't mean to dinner, either, but complete termination because that was what guys like that deserved. Yes, my youthful experience was wide and varied and was a big difference to your normal 11 year old. But I loved every minute of it.

My nickname was to change again with my ever increasing involvement with the sound system world. I was now known as **Big Youth**. This name was given to me by Soferno-B, himself, after the popular deejay by said name, because I could talk musical lyrics on the microphone very well at this young age – they called it **toasting**, then. I won my first deejay contest at the age of ten-plus at the **Telegraph Pub** in Brixton Hill, deejaying on **Duke Reid's** sound, which was the resident system every Sunday night.

There was a deejay called U-Roy on Duke Reid's sound who sounded identical to the world famous **U-Roy** from Jamaica, and week after week no one could defeat him. I decided I was going to take him and several others on. Can you imagine this little boy challenging these top-notch deejays? First of all I should never have been allowed in because I was not even old enough to be on the premises where alcohol was being sold. Secondly, what could I bring to the table to topple these popular deejays? Do re-live that night with me:

My heart is pounding extra fast, sweat is pouring from my forehead as I wait to take to the stage. The compère calls me on. There is total silence from the crowd, waiting to hear what I am going to say as the deejay sets up my music on the turntable. The track starts and I launch full assault into my set: "...AS THE FARMER SAID TO THE POTATO/ I PLANT YOU NOW AND EAT YOU LATER/ WHO SAYS A SMALL AXE CAN'T FALL AH BIG TREE/ WATCH WHAT THIS YOUTH IS GOING TO DO TO THESE BIG GUYS YOU SEE..."

The place erupted with the crowd shouting my name. I had arrived in the deejay world and had won my first deejay competition. For this victory I was awarded 10 pounds (£10), which my bigger brother relieved me of immediately, saying he is my manager; right con artist... I successfully defended my run for a further two weeks before they decided that my time was up. Wow, what an experience! This was yet again another adult venue that I should not have been in but I hungered for this way of life and pursued every opportunity I could get to learn the sound business and the adult way of life. It was like a drug, I wanted more and more and nothing was going to stop me from getting it.

If I thought the 1960s had shown me a lot and was full of experience for me, I was in for a bag of revelations in the 70s. My exposure to adult life and mentality just grew and grew and I was practically an adult in a child's body. After moving from Somerleyton Road we moved to **2c Loughborough Park**, into one of those ghastly prefabricated houses. Let me describe these prefabs for those of you who, for whatever reason, do not know them, or if you have simply forgotten. They came in two sections and were transported on the back of some massive construction trucks. They would then be placed on some paving slabs and joined together to make three-bedroom houses, which to me more resembled dog kennels. They were also used on construction sites for offices or as canteens for workers. I hated living in them.

By this time, and being rooted amongst Soferno-B, I was slowly but surely learning my trade, waiting for the moment when I would take full control. The vibes in Brixton were changing; a lot of American influence was apparent within society, and gangs had now become territorial. Unlike today, Brixton youths had always been looked upon by the others in surrounding areas as leading the way, whether it was in fashion or the hardcore (criminal) element. The multiracial presence was also beginning to increase rapidly.

Chapter 3

THE FRONTLINE

They say the world trade centre is in America, but I say this was not so in the 1970s; it was right on **Railton Road** – known then as the **Frontline,** after moving location from Somerleyton Road. The 70s was a very different era, and never in the history of London would one single road be known for its day to day existence, even in some remote parts of the world. I called it the Line University; it was where I learnt everything about hustling and self employment from some well qualified teachers. I was faced with balancing the positive elements from the negative. I could have gone completely off the rails because when you are exposed to certain negative elements at that young age, you become so vulnerable. Some of my friends enrolled in the wrong classes. Allow me to shed some light on this. There was hardly a class that I did not try but I am glad about the ones that I didn't. In the classic film story of Oliver Twist with Fagan's den of young thieves, they sang, "You got to pick a pocket, or two, boy..." Well, in the case of some of my friends, it was not one or two – it was more like hundreds. Many of them became known as "sticks man", or professional pickpockets. The two favourite places for plying their trade were on the underground tube trains and at bus stops. There are untold amount of negative things I had done in my early days, but stealing and robbery were not amongst them. I was so anti them that I willingly passed up a great opportunity to steal some valuable goods. A close friend at secondary school had gotten hold of the keys for the AVA room. This room was where all of the audio-visual, the television and recording equipment, and other valuable items were kept. He wanted us to break in and steal some of this equipment but it was obvious he did not know me as well as he thought he did, because if he did he would never have approached me with this proposal. He could have suggested many other wrong things to do and knowing myself at that time, I would have been led to take the risk. But from my younger days to present times, stealing and robbery were never in my portfolio. I felt so angry that he'd approached me that I immediately parted friendship with this long time friend and for over twenty years I did not speak to him.

The shop premises which were occupied by white English shop keepers had slowly changed hands. For example, Hackmans Newsagents and sweet shop became **Eggys'** shop. He managed it more as a sweet and grocery shop downstairs, while the upstairs became the venue for regular blues dances, where SOFERNO-B would play. Later on the premises became owned by **Tumpa.** Both he and Eggys were original back in the day Brixton men. The blues would not start fully until late, around 3am Sunday morning, for two main reasons. Firstly, the younger set of ravers (punters) would go to the **Ace Cinema** along the Brixton Hill road, where every Saturday was late night pictures (cinema). The 70s saw **martial arts** mania sweep England and it was those films that we went to watch before going to the local blues dance. There were classic movies like **Snuff Bottle Connection, Return of Mantis, Iron Fist, Eagles Claw, Fist of Fury, Snake in the Eagle's Shadow,** and characters such as **Silver Fox, Wung Chu** and the legendary **Bruce Lee**. The Ace Cinema subsequently became the Fridge and is now called Electric Brixton.

The other reason for the late start of the blues was the elite rude boys. Top players like them always went to the West End to do their thing before coming to the blues dance, which could be putting their girls to work or checking on them engaging in prostitution or supplying drugs in the night clubs. By then they would have a considerable amount of cash on them, ready to purchase champagne, brandy or Bacardi rum all night long, and also cocaine for the few who were taking cocaine at that time, even though the majority smoked weed (cannabis) and hash. In those days most of the fellows who smoked drugs favoured the more expensive black hash (or hashish – the resin made from the buds and top leaves of the weed). I remember struggling with the potent smell of it and the burning sensation that my eyes felt. I then tried the weed itself later on, even though I told myself that I would never smoke this stuff – yeah, right. I might not have started to experiment with it in my early days, compared to some, having started at the age of nineteen, but when I did start I made up for lost time. You want to know about being an herb smoker? Just continue reading my story.

Who can forget number **45 Railton Road**, down the basement? No windows down there and only one way in and the same way out, six nights a week. This was another of Soferno-B's resident venues. Theses types of places were not for the faint hearted, let alone a youngster (teenager) like me. At any moment anything could have happen, so there was always an element of mystery in the air. For one thing, it could have been raided by the police at anytime, or an act of violence could have been displayed by the hardcore hustlers and villains. The shop above it was run by two characters called **Tarp** and **Henry**. You could buy bun and cheese, fry fish (fried fish), and something which I use to love, **snowball**, which was shaved ice with syrup over it. The favourite drink for the adults was **Bacardi Rum**, chased with **Lucozade.** Because there were no windows in the basement, the only way you would know if it was daylight was when you surfaced, climbing up those steep stairs. What an atmosphere.

During the years Brixton had some unscrupulous police officers, and at the time of 45 Railton Road, there was a woman inspector in charge of Brixton; we called her **Hitler's Daughter.** She was so full of herself even some of her own officers did not like her. She had a point to prove in a male dominated environment and she was not taking any prisoners. Normally if the police came into a blues or shub-in, it was in numbers, just in case. Not so with Hitler's Daughter. I can remember clearly she walked into number 45 one night, accompanied only by one other officer. She wanted to let us know that she ruled the roost. One of the local bad boys threw a Lucozade bottle at her and it crashed against the wall. She did not blink or show any fear, which I found so remarkable I can still remember it as if it was yesterday.

These were her words, "So you're throwing bottles at me, I will be back in ten minutes; let me see you throw bottles then." True to her word she returned in ten minutes, but this time with what appeared to be the whole of Brixton police station, plus dogs. But by this time the only persons that were there was myself and the others that were responsible for the sound system. She smiled and said, "That's better, and make sure you don't play another record for the night otherwise you will be playing in the station in a cell." One mean lady. Because she was in power she terrorised Brixton during her reign. I witnessed many incidents, especially on the Frontline where she was always in the thick of things. She would drive slowly up and down the road in broad daylight, observing the hustlers. I had seen her again many times on her own.

There was only one occasion on which she actually spoke to me and this was in a blues dance on Mayall Road, directly behind Railton Road. She raided the blues and I was standing by the sound. She came over to me and, unknown to me, there was a packet of weed cannabis which someone had quickly discarded from their pocket onto the floor. Trust eagle eyes to see it whilst I remained unaware of it. She bent down and picked up the packet, waved it in front of my face, and said, "This is yours." I wanted to answer her in an unfavourable way but I knew if I did, she would have arrested or harassed me so I calmly said no. She looked at me with those penetrating eyes without saying a word for a few seconds, checking to see if I was nervous, then finally she handed the parcel to one of the officers. Yet again another dance had been ruined by Hitler's Daughter and she felt good. The reign of terror by this non-fearing woman went on for about a year before they gave her promotion and moved her on.

Among the racist detectives who stalked the streets of Brixton in the early 70s was **The Runner**. He was a slim and very tall plain clothes officer who always wore trainers. He was a nasty piece of work who, although we crossed paths on many occasions, thankfully never nicked me. However, I remember him grilling me one day, just dying to find an excuse to slap the cuffs on me. It was no use trying to run away from him for he was very athletic and would chase you on foot, no matter the distance, until you dropped from exhaustion. Next up was a detective called **Savage**. I need say no more, the name spoke for itself. When he arrested you, it was not only the handcuffs he would be putting on you. Taking advantage of his size, he was built like a rugby player, he would beat you first and then read you your rights afterwards. I knew many youths, the majority of them slightly older than myself, who got a battering from this plain clothes officer. Thankfully, I did not. These officers drove Rover V8 cars and were frequent visitors on the Frontline, targeting the hardcore youths and the main villains and hustlers.

The main eating place on the Frontline was none other than **Peggy's Restaurant** which, in the latter days, moved further down onto Atlantic Road. This is where one could get proper yard (Jamaican) food. Later on in the 70s, **Broderick's** opened on the opposite side of the Frontline to Peggy's. Broderick's was one of the first Caribbean take-away shops – you name it he sold it. Also on the corner of Barnwell Road and Railton Road you had the **Palm Tree Restaurant.**

If you were keeping a dance, a christening or a wedding, you'd visit **Bangees Off Licence** where you could get a consignment of drinks on sale-or-return. If you were after parts for your car, **Railton Spares** on the corner of Leeson Road and Railton Road was a popular choice.

They are now currently at Brixton Hill, still owned by the original owners.

Among the popular shops on the Frontline was a **bookie's** (betting shop) called **James Lane**. Caribbeans liked to have a flutter on the horses and nothing has really changed over the years concerning this contagious habit. The amount of lives and marriages I have witnessed being destroyed by this disease is distressing. The victims who fell prey to this bug often did not make it home with their wage packets, that is, if they were in regular employment, thus leaving their homes short of income. Then there were the others for whom the booking shop was their place of employment, so to speak (the professional gambler or the drug dealer). However, the problem I saw with this race horse gambling was that they were forever trying to win back what they had lost on the previous race but nine out of ten times they ended up being the loser, for some of these bets were for huge amount of cash.

This unwise indulgence is still gravitated to by many in these times and I still see some of the characters who were doing this back in the 70s, still hanging out in the betting shops. Many are grand and great grand fathers who should be setting a better example but they are mixing there with the younger set of men, often finding themselves in confrontational situations in which they should not be. And it is mostly my Black brothers who are there in their masses. You can count the white males in there on one hand, if that. Again, I know what I am saying here is going to cause offence to some, but this book is about the truth. Las Vegas had nothing on "The Line"; you were spoilt for choice of gambling houses. In fact, almost whatever you needed could be supplied on a 24-hour Frontline that never slept.

The attention which I should have been paying to my school work was not there. Nevertheless, I did reasonably well in life owing to my love for the sound system and music. At this stage my expertise on street life was vastly expanded. I was beginning to have full understanding of hardcore hustling. There were some women I knew that had headed for Europe to offer their services for a price and every so often they would return to Brixton, showing off their ill-gotten gains. Some of the men I was amongst did not realize I knew the fullness of what was going on, even though they knew I was pretty much clued up for my age. Some of theses foxy ladies were ones who were no longer working for the guys; that was their way of escaping from their pimps. This was where girl power started, not with the Spice Girls.

The youth club which I mentioned earlier on, Shepherd's on Railton Road, was allowed, from the 1970s, to play sound system music and they quickly became a focal point for it. Sound systems like Soferno-B, my sound, and others like Neville King, were allowed to play there on a regular basis. Every Monday was our slot and the number one selector on Soferno-B then was **Denzil**, one of the best selectors of that era – around 1972. He was the complete selector, meaning he was good at both chatting on the mike and throwing down a crucial selection at the same time. I watched him closely for I was learning my trade from him. As far as I was concerned, only the great **Festus**, who played on Coxsone sound, could rival him, and he would give Festus trouble whenever they encountered each other in dances. I was just waiting patiently for my time to come, which I did not know was very near.

Now that Denzil was at the peak of his popularity, he was highly sought after by his female fan base. I can clearly remember saving him from a fatal injury one night. In those days the sound system selectors would select with their backs to the crowd, occasionally turning around to see what the reaction of the crowd was, or to speak to a dance punter. One of Denzil's girlfriends was making her way forward to plunge a knife into him. Quickly, I alerted him, which saved him from being stabbed in his back. The dance nearly came to an end as he set about her in his retaliation. Even though she was wrong, I felt sorry for her because she received a severe battering. Denzil was also a very outspoken person, which led to personality clashes at the best of times between himself and the owner of Soferno-B sound system. One Saturday night we were packing away the sound in the van after playing at a blues dance in Mostyn Road. As we came up from the basement, one of the speaker boxes got damaged.

The Soferno-B himself was not there, as he was pursuing his regular profession, which was chauffeuring, so he did not know about the damage to the speaker. Denzil should have informed him of this but he did not, so it was not until we were taking out the sound to play at Shepherd's club on the Monday that Soferno-B knew what had happened. Well, no need to say, he was not pleased. Now Denzil, being the big selector, always arrived after we had done the donkey work of lifting the boxes. However, this time when he turned up there was a big argument between him and B and they both decided to call their relationship a day. Soferno-B then turned to me and said, "It's your time now, you are in full control." Just like that. I entered the job in full flight and was determined to take this sound to another level within time, and that was exactly what I did.

Chapter 4

ANOTHER LEVEL

Now this other level I was entering into was wide in more ways than you can imagine. This was the mid 70s and things were moving on rapidly. In the sound system world you had to be on top of your game or no bookings, which we called dates, would be coming in.

There were quite a few new sounds entering the scene from all areas, wanting to make their impact, so this was not a time for being complacent. Therefore, with my experience and enthusiasm I set to work of taking Soferno-B to another level. To name a few of the sounds that started to emerge, you had **King Tubby's, Moa Ambassa, Supertone, Small Axe,** and **Saxon**, all from south London, in addition to those from the other areas of London and the country in general. The country sounds came mainly from the midlands and north of England which, over the years, have produced some credible sounds such as the great **Quaker City, Mafia Tone,** and **Jungle Man,** who all lined up to claim the scalp of one of the top London sounds.

I started to drive at the age of 16 and I passed my driving test at 17, in December 1975. I was still attending school when I was not too tired from playing sound system the night before. Even from this time I knew a lot of the big weed dealers but I still had not started smoking as yet. However, from the business side of it, I understood the financial gain which could be achieved; but was I willing to get involved? A big man named Mosa called me one day and said, "I have been watching you long time and you are a smart youth. Do you know that I can make you make some serious money?" By this time many youngsters were into smoking weed, even some of my sixth form friends, so this could have been the door opened for me to start supplying. However, my love of sound system was greater and at that stage I was not prepared to take the risk.

I stayed on until the sixth form and was the first youth among my peers to be driving to school, often picking up some of my school mates. Well, you can imagine the jealousy being thrown at me from all sides. My first car my Mum brought me was a Ford Corsair 1.7 engine, followed shortly after that by a new Ford Capri. One day when I drove into school the headmaster called me to his office and told me that I could not park my car on the school premises anymore. The real problem there was that some of the teachers felt offended because this little Black student was driving a better car than the teachers so I had to start parking out on the road. No big deal, because they could not stop me from driving.

I stayed on and took a few O-level exams, which I passed, and it was now time to fully enter the big bad world. Thank the Good Lord, He had somewhat prepared me for what was to come, although I was not aware of this. Now at this time Soferno-B had a regular spot at a venue called **Ravers 78**, where we played on Friday and Saturday nights, if we did not have other bookings. The number 78 referred to the door number, not the year, and it was situated at Grange Road in Bermondsey. We would play alongside a sound called **Rootsman** which was owned by a cool brother called David. We got on well even though we were more popular than they were.

This is something else I must mention; I was one of the first to play a Beres Hammond selection in England, from back in the early blues dances. The tune we made famous with him on Soferno-B sound was called *I Wish I Had a Dream*. All ravers from back in that time can verify that. No sound was playing Beres then. He used to entertain tourists on the North Coast in Jamaica, singing mostly as a cabaret entertainer but I knew from then that he would be a major recording artist. Yet you have certain sound selectors trying to discredit me and going on as if they were the first to play certain artists when I was always a pioneer in playing music and promoting certain unknown artists at the time. Do you remember tunes like *Sweetie Come From America* by Well Pleased & Satisfied; *Sunday Coming,* by Alton Ellis; *Heart and Soul* by Junior Byles; *Mrs Brown,* by Jacob Miller; *Picture on the Wall,* by Freddie McKay, *Everything I Own,* by Ken Boothe; *My Girl,* by The Techniques; *Go Away Dream,* by Derrick Harriott; *No Funeral,* by Prince Alla; *I'm Your Puppet,* by Jimmy London; *My Baby Just Cares for Me,* by **Nina Simone***; Stop the Fussing and Fighting,* by **Culture**; *This Will Be,* by **Natalie Cole**; and *Lady of Magic,* by Bunny Malone. All of them and too many more to mention were played by me on Soferno-B and the rest of selectors would follow my blues dance selection but would give me no credit.

We were also the first sound to start playing on what was to become the popular **Boat Trip Dances** up and down the River Thames, leaving from various piers. The coach outing dances at various seaside beaches were another of Soferno-B's regular ventures, as was the clashing against other sounds.

Now here comes the change of direction: a well known and respected hardcore brother from Brixton, called Nyah Ochi, who I had known for years, decided that the sound would gain greater advantage by playing in the hood of Brixton six nights a week at what was to become the famous **Villa Road Shub-in**. The end result of this would be that the hardcore villains and the Brixton crew would embrace and follow the sound. We are talking about the "man dem" who were in control of all the runnings that took place on the Frontline, aka Railton Road. I am not talking about babies here; these were hardcore villains who did not take prisoners, wore the best clothes, drove the best cars, drank champagne and Bacardi, and what they said went. Nyah Ochi was a top general amongst them and highly respected, so our back was covered.

As I said, changes were happening fast and I was now on my way to opening my first business venture outside of music; becoming one of the youngest Black entrepreneurs in that era. At aged 20 I started running one of the most successful and nationally acclaimed night clubs, the **Bali-Hi** in Streatham. If I thought I had enemies before, then what was to come made them seem almost meaningless. Running this club was not a venture to be taken lightly for there were so many high profile and hardcore villains who would have loved and wanted to be in the position that I was so fortunate to find myself in. I often wondered when physical confrontation would kick off as some of these villains and hardcore gangsters were known to take out men for a lesser gain. There were a number of soundmen who were not pleased either, and were wondering how on earth this youth got the opportunity to run this night club. If they wanted their sound to be featured in the number one club they would have to come to me, and this made them mad.

Up to this time, over thirty years on, there are still some individuals carrying the same hate for me. Imagine, I am not even in the sound business anymore and some still hate me with a vengeance, talking all kind of things against me. This is why this book is going to make it worse but I stand by the truth. In these present times there are youths who can identify with this as they are running their ends, making money, and the haters are giving them a fight. One of the things that really annoy me is that many of them are snakes; they see me and laugh with me, saying how they respect me but by the time I walk off they return to bad mouth me with their venomous ways, in some cases cursing about what they would like to do to me. Talk about sour grapes, 'envious and bad mind'. There are a few who call themselves top class selectors who claim to be better than me, yet none of them have accomplished what I have, or have my credibility. My name for them is "jukeboxes" – they put on the record but someone has to tell them which one.

This club was right above the skating rink (which was still in operation until very recently when it was moved to Brixton). Again I can only say it was divine intervention that made me get this club. It was un-usual for someone as young as me to have such a night club at my disposal. However, I think it was due to me enjoying divine intervention in my life. Significantly, one night I walked into the club and there was a sound playing there. You could have counted the number of people there on one hand, and there was no atmosphere – the deejay was playing on the in-house system and it sounded like a transistor radio.

I made enquires as to who the manager of the club was and I was soon introduced to a man of Caribbean origin named Phil. Straight away he took an instant liking to me. I told him who I was and what vision I could see for a place like that under the right management. This pricked his ears up. The building actually belonged to Mecca Enterprises but profits for this place were at an all time low. They were not going to keep on suffering this, and his job was also on the line.

After two more meetings I put my proposals to Phil and he liked the sound of what he heard. He told me he could see a budding young entrepreneur in the making and agreed to test my potential with one night a week at first, which was a Sunday night. However, for this to work I had to get the clubbers in, and a good music system would greatly assist in this. Therefore, I just could not work with their in-house system and so I had to somehow convince him that I would have to bring in my own hi-power system, which at that time I was managing for Soferno-B.

At first he was not having this and I had to use his system. However, after two weeks I confirmed to him that it was still not working so he finally agreed. That was when **Bali-Hi club** took off! It was such a success that after a short period of time he offered me the Thursday nights as well. Here I was at the young age of 20, running a top night club for myself and making serious money with a staff of 20 employees working for me!

In the next stage of my planned development, I made Thursday nights the time for Roots music lovers. I employed the warrior sound of **Jah Shaka** to play alongside myself, and later I brought in other sounds as well − in rotation. All sound men wanted to be friends with me because I could give them work and promotion at the most talked about dance venue of that time. But more and more the knives were coming out. I was walking a tight rope without realising the full extent of this hate rage and that it was not going to be short lived. However, in no way at that time could I have anticipated that this was going to carry on for such a great number of years. It is so amazing to see the true colours of some people. You do not have to directly offend them for some to hate you with full venom, all because of your success and the lack of their own; as if it is your fault.

Since playing with Jah Shaka at **Bali-Hi**, I have subsequently engaged with him in a number of sound clashes over the years, but I remember one dance in particular at Brixton Town Hall. Now Shaka is a roots sound and I was the versatile selector who threw punches from all angles, meaning that I played a wider range of music than most sounds, even introducing the famous commercial break which was when I would change the mood with a couple of soul tunes. However, Shaka hated whenever I started to play my roots selection because I had tunes which he felt he should be playing instead of me, especially because I was not a Rasta man but a bald head, as they would say in those days. Well, this bald head took no prisoner and I had crucial selections like **Feed Back** and **Jammin**, by Al Campbell, and **I Love**

Sweet Jah Jah, by **Barry Brown.** When Shaka did eventually get Sweet Jah Jah he nearly wore it out on 12-inch disc. **Trickster** by Junior Delgado and **Slave Driver** by Dennis Brown are more examples of the 'cut' of tunes we used to play, cut for cut, in competition, until whoever ran out first, and it was never me.

In those days **Daddy Ernie** used to come and listen to me. He was my close friend and admirer who always loved it when I "destroyed" sounds. David Rodigan used to have to look up to a selector like me, often asking me about various tunes and other aspects of the business. Later on he felt he was too big to talk to a man like me. However, over the years I made a lot of sound-man earn money yet none of them have ever called me and said come and earn some money. This is why they were glad to see the back of me and also why this book is so controversial because so many truths have been revealed and if they are big enough they will all admit it.

My influence in the business was due partly to the selection of tunes I was able to get. Two other classic tunes, **Moulding**, by **I Jahman Levi** and the awesome **Weed Fields** by Desi Roots, were among many exclusives that I was the first to play. Much of my supply came from Roy, who controlled the **Hawkeye record label** and shop in Harlesden, northwest London. He gave me exclusive tunes over the years to annihilate other sounds. I should not forget the **Cha Cha** record label. They controlled all of Channel One productions from Jamaica, supplying me with selections like The Viceroy's **Heart Made of Stone**, and do not even forget my **Little Roy** and **Wailing Souls** selections. These were selections Shaka would crave for. Any Al Campbell dub which he eventually got was because I told Al to give him a cut. All told, I still respect Jah Shaka; he is a legend in the sound business and is still playing today.

It was now time to start investing some of this cash which I had made, for I am the type of person who was always trying something constructive. Another twist in this saga involved **Lloyd Coxsone**, who was one of my rivals in the sound world but he always admired me for my gifts and determination as a young youth in the business. He was also my in-law through my eldest brother who was the father of his sister's two children – it is, indeed, a small world. Lloydie Coxsone was at the time, running a record shop at Granville Arcade in Brixton and needed a partner for the business as he and his then business partner wanted to part company. Now he knew that I wanted to open a record shop for myself and he offered me the chance to join with him, with the intention that after a period of time I would buy him out. And so I agreed.

When it came to time to buy Lloydie Coxsone out, I decided to bring Soferno-B in on this deal and we agreed that all of us would take a quarter share, along with and including my long time very close friend, Neville. What I did not know was that this was going to be a bad decision as far as involving Soferno-B was concerned, but a blessing for me and Neville.

Opening the record shop was not to be my only investment from the ever growing income that I was accumulating from running **Bali-Hi** and the sound system. Another one of my dreams was to launch a successful record label producing my own rhythm tracks and voicing local and Jamaican artists. This now was to be the emergence of the **Big Youth Records** label. God had gifted me with being able to spot talent way before the individual would become a star. I knew a great singer or deejay (rapper) when I heard one. But first thing was first. For my successful recording label I needed my own in-house musicians. Another very close long time friend of mine called Raymond Simpson was a very talented musician, singer, and song-writer. He used to jam with some other musicians in the basement of his father's barber shop on Shakespeare Road a few evenings a week. I told him of my intention to launch a record label and we forged an even tighter relationship. I could not sing or play an instrument but I knew how to make great music based on having great ideas and sharp ears.

We both decided that the band needed a great name and came up with the name **Wreckless Breed**. The band consisted of a bass player called Preacher, a very talented musician but slippery as eels. The drummer was called Barrington who, together with Preacher, both played on a lot of Castro Brown productions on the DEB label, and backed many well known artists such as Gregory Isaacs, Dennis Brown, and local talent like **15-16-17**, which was an all girl teenage group, as well as a brother and sister act called **Me and You**. The keyboard player was called Harry Guy and was the brother of the great female lovers rock singer, Sandra Cross. There were some other musicians who we used to jam with, such as the famous Spunky and his brother, Earl.

My Record Label

Me, outside my record shop

Along with me on the sound I had a talented recording engineer called Fitzroy who, at that time, was applying his day trade at the **De Wolfe** Music studios in the West End's Wardour Street. He got some studio time at a reduced rate and I was ready to do my first set of rhythm tracks. Me being the type of person I was, I thought if I made my musicians comfortable in all areas they should play some wicked tracks so I laid on a big spread with food and gave them the best grade of sensimeanya (sensemilla/ganja/weed) to smoke, plus a decent session rate of pay for each of them. Big mistake.

During the session the tracks did not sound too bad but when I got home and had a closer listen, not one of them was up to standard. I learnt my first learning lesson in the recording business and went back to the drawing board, so to speak.

I quickly booked another session, this time at a bigger studio with a 24 track mixing desk, at TMC recording studios in Tooting Broadway. I told the same musicians that the only thing they would be getting from me this time was their recording session fee so they shouldn't even ask me for a sheet of Rizla. Bingo! What a difference that made. We laid down ten tracks and every one was up to the mark. I thought to myself, "Things ah gwaan now (progression is being made)!"

During these years, the mid 70s, I had some close relationships with Jamaican artists such as, my close friend **Sugar Minott** (who was also the god father to one of my sons, Shamar); such as **Dennis Brown; Junior Delgado; Heptones; Mighty Diamonds; Trinity; Dillinger; Twinkle Brothers; Clint Eastwood; Linval Thompson; Barrington Levy; Triston Palmer; Gregory Isaacs; Sammy Dread; Burning Spear; Toots and The Maytals; Jah Thomas;** and my very close friend, **Jackie Mittoo,** Jamaica's greatest keyboard player, to name but a few.

When it came to producers, I had good working relationships with the likes of the great duo, **Robbie and Sly Dunbar,** also **Bunny Lee, Niney** (of the Observer label), **Winston Riley, and Henry Junjo Laws**. I even rubbed shoulders on a couple of occasions with the legendary **Bob Marley** who caused a stampede when he turned up at **Bali-Hi** one Sunday night. You see, Bali-Hi was the place to be and it was well known within the Jamaican music world; they would all hang out there when they were in town.

I purposely left it to last to speak about my relationship with none other than Mr **Al Campbell** who, if the truth be spoken, I can claim some of the credit for helping his career to take off in England. He was not alone where that was concerned but I had a much closer relationship with him than with the other artists. For example, when he was in London, which was quite often, he would stay at my home which I shared with my Mother and younger brother. My Mum would always make him feel comfortable – on a few occasions she gave up her bedroom to accommodate him. I was blessed with the type of mother for whom nothing was too much to do for others. It is her that I got that spirit from, but more often than not I would end up being hurt or taken for granted. Anyway, Al would cut certain exclusive dubs for me whenever he was in Jamaica and New York so he was another of my exclusive music connections.

After a period of time he did a set of recordings for me (on my Big Youth Records label) and one of them is still a firm favourite in revival dances today. This was his cover version of the song, **You Know You Want To Be Loved,** which was a very good seller and my highest charted tune. Yet with all of this and without going into the ins and outs of a very long story, our friendship ended, which was sad in a way because of the respect that was shown in the earlier days.

In those days there were no pirate radio stations (or community stations, as they are known today) and reggae music being played on mainstream radio was limited, so the top sound systems were the means of promoting reggae music. Accordingly, if your tune was being featured at Bali-Hi club, or any of the many other venues that I would play all over England, it was getting a wide listening audience.

Let me tell you about one of the many horrifying experiences I had at that time. We had just finished playing at Bali-Hi one Sunday night and went on, as usual, to play in a blues dance. This particular house dance I am going to tell you about was taking place at St. John's Crescent in Brixton, near to the police station on Gresham Road. The price to gain entry in those days was one pound (£1.00). Some youths from outside the area wanted to come into but it seemed they did not want to pay or they did not have enough money. The door man, who I knew very well, told the youths on several occasions to either pay or move from the gate, but they did neither. After telling them one final time, the youths still refused to cooperate and a big argument broke out between them and the doorman. Now I and one of the other soundmen were standing at the bottom of the stairs which led to the door so we both saw everything that took place.

By now the argument between the doorman and the youths had become intense and it eventually lead to him and one of them starting to fight. Now this doorman was not one to take prisoners and he pulled out his knife. They got hold of each other and both fell down the stairs. When they landed the youth fell on the knife which the doorman had.

The youth panicked and ran off, blood pouring out of his wound, but he did not get very far because he passed out round the corner. It seemed like it was time to get the hell out of there so I rushed inside and told my understudy who was playing the sound to lock off quickly and let us pack up the sound. Now because of the rush the truck was not packed correctly – we just chucked the equipment in to make a fast escape but the back door couldn't close.

The next thing we heard were sirens blazing and we saw the blue flashing lights of the police vehicles. A voice shouted: "NOBODY MOVE, EVRYONE BACK INSIDE THE HOUSE! At this time the doorman and all but three of the dance punters had already left the scene. Only I, Soferno-B and the rest of the crew, plus the three dance punters remained there. The police officer who was in charge started to make some inquiries of us then he got a call on his radio: "THE YOUTH WHO GOT STABBED HAS DIED ON THE WAY TO HOSPITAL." The officer then said to us, "Right, you are all going down to the station; this is now a murder inquiry."

Now remember what I said, that I witnessed all that had taken place. They loaded us all into the back of the police vans, and being nearby we arrived at the station in no time. The police split us up and divided us into two cells. Things were now getting even more tense and one of the officers said, "Right, we want a statement from each of you," and one by one they took us out of the cells to give our statements.

After about four persons had given their statements, it was now my turn. What was I going to say, that I saw everything, plus I knew the doorman well? The only statement they were going to get from me was that I did not see anything. The police wanted to know everything I did that day, from in the afternoon until the time they detained me. All kinds of things were running through my head, wondering what the outcome of this would be. Anyway, I told them that I saw nothing and signed my statement, after which they put me back in the cell. I asked my friend, who also saw everything, what he told them and he said the same as me. After about three hours, guess who walked into the cell area, accompanied by two officers? None other than the doorman who unintentionally stabbed the youth. My heart sunk. Remember, I had just told the police that I did not see anything. What if he tells them I am his witness? Perjury, right? Whatever the charge, it would certainly concern withholding vital information in a murder inquiry. I was certainly in one of those "somebody get me some toilet paper", situations.

The police interviewed him and an officer who was guarding us (because they had left the cell door open) said, as they passed by with the doorman, "There he is, that's who done the murder." By this time I am feeling numb. They did not let me out until about 3pm the next day, by which time my Mother was in a state of total worry, not seeing me come home and knowing that anything could have happened, because my lifestyle and the music business carried certain risk elements.

They had by now charged the doorman with murder and he was on remand in Brixton Prison. He sent me a message via a friend of mine, saying that he needed to speak to me urgently for he had not made a statement yet and wanted to know what I had said before he did so. I arranged a visit and I told him that I had told them that I did not see anything. He then decided that he was not going to call me as a witness and it would be just his word against the Prosecution's.

I felt that God was guiding me into fulfilling His calling for me later on in my life and this was all part of my training. The doorman was eventually found guilty of manslaughter and got seven years. This was just one of the many unsavoury incidents I witnessed in my days on Soferno-B sound. I have seen certain gangsters beat both their girlfriends and other men senseless on several occasions, sending chills down my spine. For example, one night Sharper was in the blues dance with one of his many girls and another one of his girls showed up and started to create a scene. He just pulled her into the bathroom and all we could hear was loud screaming. After a few minutes he came out with his knife in his hand, wiping blood off with his handkerchief. Her friends rush into the bathroom to find her in a pool of blood lying on the floor. She had a pair of white trousers on when she went in but it was now red. And you know, the madness about this was that a few weeks after this she was back in the dance with him. And this was just a tip of the iceberg. If I was to write about the many more that I have witnessed there would be no room for the rest of my story so let's move unto something more pleasant.

As a selector you have to be able to use psychology over your opponents, and this was another gift I had. Let me give you this lick. I was playing against **Moa Ambassa** one Friday night at **St Giles** club in Camberwell and their owner/selector, **Berris**, was running off his mouth as usual. I said to myself that I am going to put a stop to this once and for all. My then boss, Soferno-B, had just recently returned from Jamaica armed with some serious dub plates (exclusive tunes) but I did not bother to bring them with me that night, thinking that it was no big deal and that I would save them for another time. Well, that was a mistake, for Berris was getting seriously 'out of order' and anyone who knows me knows I don't take cheek. So I took up my mike and said to Berris, "Give me twenty minutes to go to my house and come back and see if I don't rip you to pieces." Surprisingly, Berris accepted my request.

I turned off the sound and jumped into the sound truck. I lived on the Angell Town Estate, not far away, and I don't know how the truck did not turn over with the speed I was going. I grabbed the dubs and hurried straight back. You could feel the tension as I walked back into the crowd, who waited eagerly – never had they witnessed something like this before.

I lined up the first dub plate. It was the first time this Dennis Brown track was going to be heard in England and this track was also to become one of his classic hits. I put the disc on and lined up the needle... "Fresh out of **Joe Gibbs'** studio," and the crowd heard, **"Money In My Pocket But I Just Can't Get No Love..."** They erupted into pure jubilation! The next right upper cut I gave Berris was another big tune called **By The Look In Your Eyes** by **Enos McLeod**. By this time Berris was wishing he could just disappear, along with his crew and sound. The last track I finished him off with was a big tune by **Pat Kelly**, a track called **Jammin**. All of these tunes were fresh and never heard before. They were too much for **Moa**

Ambassa sound and he got the first of several beatings I was going to dish out to him.

Now I could never find myself in such a position because if that were me, I would not be underrating anyone by giving them permission to leave the dance – you'd better stay there and defend it. And this was how **Chabba Melo** used to flex back in my sound days.

The place I would go to cut my Dub plates was the famous **John Hassell Recordings** studio, which was at 21 Nassau Road, Barnes, south west London. John Hassell was a senior-aged white man who in his earlier days was a sound engineer at the BBC. He set up a Dub cutting room in the front room of his house and this became the more favoured dub cutting studio for most of the big soundman then. Many times I would meet up by chance with my rivals, including Coxsone, Shaka, and Moa Ambassa, cutting their dubs there. It was often a drama with whoever was cutting first and did not want his rival to hear his selection. As a rule, therefore, we would wait in our cars until the other was finished. John Hassell's wife, called Felicity, would also cut the dubs if John was ill or not available and she knew tunes, too. John Hassell lived in a residential area with middle and upper class neighbours, so you can imagine some strange looks we received when we pulled up outside his house. John was a great man and over the years we got on well, treating each other with respect and consideration.

The two other cutting rooms that I also used sometimes were **Terry** over at St John's Wood and, later on, **Chris** over at Holloway Road, but John was the main man.

Now back to the blessing for myself and Neville which I mentioned earlier on. I regarded Soferno-B as a father figure, especially as I was not raised by my own biological Father and had grown up amongst him. I always had the utmost respect for him and I thought that he was thrilled for me as his young protégé making successful advancement at my young age. But how wrong I was; to my greatest surprise there was resentment there – what Jamaicans would call **bad mind** (envy).

After bringing B in on my business venture, things were cool at first and before long the record shop was running things in Brixton. Soon, our rivals such as Desmond Hip City on Atlantic Road; Larry Lawrence's shop, Ethnic Fight on Coldharbour Lane; and Junior Booth's shop, JB'S on Acre Lane, were all put under pressure by our performance. When it came to getting the latest tunes, there was only one shop in control and all the other sound system and deejays came to our shop. I even allowed it to be named **Soferno-B Record Shack** because as far as I was concerned, B was my mentor and father figure. But the younger customers thought that I was Soferno-B because it was me they would always see.

We had the greatest record salesman of that era working for us. He was one of Sir Coxsone's original sound man, named Michael, like myself, but he was better known as **Scotty** or **Screwface**. Scotty could sell you a tune even if you did not like it, he was that good. He would approach you with sheer psychology and you were not leaving our shop without making a purchase. Later on I also employed another great record shop salesman – the one and only George, aka Nasty Rocker, who was a firm favourite with our senior clientele.

This is where I have to clear up another longstanding issue in the sound system business. **Sir Coxsone** is a sound I have the most respect for. Coxsone sound is a legendary sound, a pioneer in the sound system business in the UK and when I speak of Coxsone I am talking about the original crew. For those who do not know, here we go: you had **Lloyd Coxsone**, himself; Festus, one of the greatest selectors to play sound system; Gunsmoke; Byron; Castro Brown, who later built his own sound; also, Morpheus; Sport; Mr. C aka Clarence, and his brother, Scotty; Junior Booth, who owned JB record shop on Acre Lane; Glen, who was also co-owner of the record shop; Trevor, aka Sanatone; and Miser. These were the men I grew up knowing and seeing round Coxsone Sound. However, it is the later crew that many of you will be familiar with, men like, Blacker Dread; Duffus; Skeeroy; Jah Lloyd; Naptali; Country, aka Levi Roots; Natty; Peebles; Harlesden; Bikey Dread; Dego; OneDan; Gappy; and Hawk, who used to drive their truck. Now don't get me wrong, I have due regard for the later crew, but compared to my experience in the sound business their history is in the later class.

Now there was one person in their original crew that I really admired. When I was growing up and just started to play sound, Festus was my idol. As a selector he would destroy other selectors, just like a Mike Tyson of the sound business. What he did not realize was that I was studying him, waiting for my time to take his crown, and it came one night in Bali-Hi club. It was a Sunday and we had played Coxsone's crew in a football match at Brockwell Park. Our crew, Soferno-B, beat them 9-0. They were still upset when our sounds played each other that night at Bali-Hi. Festus decided – or should I say, thought, he was going to get revenge on me through the sound. Wrong move... Not only did he get beat up in the football, he was now going to get it through the sound as well.

When we got to Bali-Hi, Festus told his crew to bring in the entire sound because he was going to kill me. What he did not know was that it was he who was going to die with his undisputed title gone. We started to play and he played a Gregory Isaacs tune called Mrs Brown, which he tried to hype-up by saying it was a Canadian mix. Sugar Minott had given me a barrage of tunes to destroy any sound that tested us. I remember it like yesterday and this is how I punished him. I played a brand new dub by Sugar Minott called African Girl and if you know your tunes you will remember how crucial that was on an upbeat lick of the famous *Shank I Sheck* rhythm.

Along with various other tunes, I started to deliver the head shots. By this time Festus was really mad but he made matters worse for himself; he sealed his own coffin when he grabbed the microphone and said, "Go suck your…" I think you get the picture. Well, although this dirty, foul-mouth profanity is unfortunately common nowadays, in those days you did not say things like that because it could end in some serious war. The whole dance turned against him, even some of his own crew members. Lloyd Coxsone scolded him, "Shame on you, Festus, you let Big Youth play music on you and then you resort to that." Lloydie was embarrassed. So that was the night I took Festus apart. I know he would not admit it but there were hundreds of witnesses, and his title was gone.

Absolutely no sound in the UK could ever have the exclusive Sugar Minott selections I used to play, and those were in the days when Sugar was storming the place. This was true for my selections on Soferno-B, and then when I had my own sound, Stereograph, as well as later on when I moved to Jamaica and ran my own sound called Destiny. That Sugar's own sound, **Youth Promotion**, did not have my exclusive Sugar Minott selections shows how close he and I were.

These are things that were never told or admitted and this is why I had to speak the truth and clear up the story because the haters never did, and still don't, to this, day give me my credit as a credible selector, no matter how many of them I proved myself against.

As I said, when I first partnered Lloyd Coxsone with the shop, he was already running it so when I took over he continued working there full time. Later on he also ran the **Big Apple** boutique on Acre Lane for Danny King who was also a sound man from back in the day. This boutique specialised in selling American clothing, especially hats, and the one all the 'ranking' would seek, the Beavers.

At first Neville and I would handle day to day operation of the shop because Soferno-B was still doing his chauffeuring job. But then it got to a stage where I can only say he felt he should be in full control and he thought he was the main man. The original plan was that I would be in total control, running the sound and the shop, but then B's ego kicked in.

After a period of time Soferno-B came to me and said that he felt it would be better if I ran the sound and he would take charge of the shop because in his eyes my main interest was the sound. Initially, I thought, what a cheek, but the reality was that I was madly in love with the sound business. I agreed to his suggestion as long as he did not interfere with the running of the sound. At first this worked fine but then the situation became too much for him, being that he was the big man (the senior) not wanting to have this little youth, his former student, running things and hogging the limelight. Increasingly, he kept interfering with my decisions so I reminded him of the agreement we had and made it clear that he could not keep on meddling in my running of the sound. No need to say that this put a great strain on our relationship and I realised that it would soon be time to move to another level and on to the blessing which I mentioned earlier.

Neville and I were always tight and he felt the same way as me. We were going to take a bad situation and turn it around to become positive. The only thing with that was that at the time we did not know what the outcome was going to be. This only became apparent after a period of time. God's doing often just does not line up with man's natural thinking and this is why He is Almighty God and He alone.

The situation with Soferno-B went on for some time and I was getting more frustrated each day. Another thing I must mention is that in those days I did not keep a car for longer than a year because, as the youngsters nowadays call it, I was making P's (paper/money) and I drove the latest and best in those days. There are many who know and can testify to what I am saying and that was another thing which irritated Soferno-B – this youth is too hot. Things were getting to breaking point and I had always dreamt of owning my own champion sound; nothing was going to stop me from achieving my dreams now. I felt it was time again to move to another level, but this had to be done clinically and precisely because I am not a person who does things in half measures – I go the full one hundred.

Let me pause here to clarify the truth about a long time dispute that arose between me and one of my rival sounds, non other than **Frontline Sound**. At that time, Soferno-B, without a shadow of a doubt, had the south London blues-dance scene under control. No other sound could test us. Now remember earlier on I mentioned certain gangsters who controlled south London, especially Brixton. They were comrades of Nyah Ochi and they were fully backing Soferno-B in the sense that this was the sound they would rave to. In addition, whenever they kept dances for themselves, we were the sound they would hire. These men carried a massive influence and many others wanted to be seen mixing in their company. In any case, you did not want to be on the wrong side of these people. The main 'baller' in the team was no other than the fearsome **Sharper.** "Dem man run things then", but let us not forget, even Sharper had great respect for our general, Nyah Ochi.

Now if you wanted to book the sound for a date you would have to go to Nyah Ochi and he would check availability with myself and give you the next available date. Well, the hardcore gangsters felt they had a divine right, that they could just come and say next week is my dance, regardless of prior bookings. They were so used to controlling everything but they did not bargain for Nyah Ochi. He was having none of this and because he was well in with them, and was a force to be reckoned with, feelings were beginning to surface over this issue.

The top dog decided that this could not go on and he was going to boycott Soferno-B sound, especially also because Soferno-B himself was not one of the boys who hustled on the streets with them. Henceforth, they decided they were going to spend their money amongst their own and, at the same time, have someone whom they could have more control over.

Now this is how **Frontline Sound** was going to enter into the picture. One of the local man off the Frontline, aka Railton Road, who rubbed shoulders with the same hardcore, decided he was going to build a sound. He always used to rave at our dances but now he felt he had the knowledge to build up a sound and call it Frontline. This was supposed to be the perfect substitute for Soferno-B and you know that in life some people are like sheep; they just follow where they think it is cool to be seen. Therefore, when the top gangsters decided to support one of their own, quite a few of the dance punters followed.

All of sudden this little sound, which had poor sound quality, was being hyped up, and the owner and his crew believed the hype. As they would say in Jamaica, they were **never-see-come-see** (not used to being or having something which gains the attention of others) and they started to act as if they were the greatest thing since sliced bread. However, the true music connoisseur knew that Frontline Sound could never be compared to Soferno-B, hence why Soferno-B sound is legendary and Frontline is not.

One evening Soferno-B called a business meeting between the three of us at his house. Little did I know what was about to emerge. We arrived about 8pm and gathered in his front room. Soferno-B poured himself a large brandy, while Neville and I, as far as I can remember, must have had a soft drink since we did not drink alcohol. With a smug look on his face he said that in his opinion, Neville and I were not showing enough interest in the shop and because of this he was putting a proposal to buy us out and take full control. Now remember, this was the man that I had brought into the business.

There was total silence in the room for a few minuets and you could cut the proverbial atmosphere with a knife. I looked at Neville and Neville looked at me in total disbelief. B then continued to state how he proposed to pay us off. If I had any doubts before, it was now clear that it was time to leave Soferno-B. We both thought about it and said as long as we got what was due to us, he could go ahead. But there are some old sayings, such as, "every unfair game is played twice", and "he who laughs last laughs best".

THE DARK SIDE OF THE SOUND BUSINESS EXPLAINED

Everything in life has two sides to it and the sound business is no different. I have experienced it from all angles, from the ins and the outs – in other words, totally. Here are a few tales from my recollection, concerning promoters of no conscience who set out to abuse and rob people.

The first one I am going to tell you about happened in the late 1970s, while I was still playing Soferno-B sound. We played at a big stage show and dance over at Hammersmith in a hotel. The artists who were performing were Al Campbell, Clint Eastwood and General Saint, Triston Palmer, and some UK artists, Trevor Walters, and Aswad. There was a good turnout and a substantial amount of cash taken in ticket sales, plus what was taken at the door on the night. After the show was over we all went to collect payment from the promoter who was a man called Dr Vernal Himes (name changed).

When I went into the hotel office this man was telling us that there was no money to pay us. I do not know if Aswad was paid prior to the show but me, Al Campbell, Clint Eastwood, General Saint and Triston Palmer were not. After some initial argument we bundled him into my car and drove him back to his office which was near Wandsworth Bridge. We manhandled him and tied him to a chair before we started to interrogate him. At this time I remember wondering how much more of the beating he could take, considering that he seemed to be of senior years. All of a sudden the door flew open and it was the police. Someone at the hotel had told them that we had kidnapped him. Again by the grace of God they did not charge us but we did not get paid.

The next incident concerned a promoter who booked me to play in Bristol. I had only taken part payment, with an agreement for the outstanding balance to be paid on the night. After driving all the way from London and playing all night, this promoter was telling me that he did not have any money to pay the balance. It was not that no one turned up to support the dance, for it was nearly full, but some of these so called dance promoters where rip-off merchants, or so they thought. I remember me and Neville telling him that we were giving him one more chance to pay up or we were going to turn the sound crew loose on him.

Now we used to have some men in the crew who did not joke and would rip him apart. **Moa Ambassa** could testify to this, if Berris wished to. They got out of order one night while we were playing them and I Spy in Wandsworth Town Hall where a promoter called Bengi used to keep regular dances. **Moa Ambassa** came late and I gave him time to do a sound check after he assembled his sound. After a period of time Berris started to act as if he wanted to take over. Well in those days you could not do that with us, you would be asking for serious trouble. Anyhow, I appealed to them to remember that we were not some little sound, and that he was playing against us so he should think about the consequences. Now then, if you knew Berris Bassa well you would know he loved to hype and he started to do that against us. My crew went over to them and all hell broke loose. **Moa Ambassa** crew had to flee – I had to stop members of my crew from inflicting some serious pain on them.

So because this promoter in Bristol did not reckon on consequence like that, he was still saying that he did not have any more money to pay us. We just turned the crew loose. The first thing they did was to strip the bar of all remaining drinks and fixtures. Then they dismantled the hall. Well, by now this damn liar of a promoter started to beg me and Neville to call them off and then he went to a safe in an office and produced the balance of our cash.

The last story I shall relate concerns a booking at Brixton Town Hall. Prior to this booking, I had one to play at **Roxy Theatre** over at Harlesden. How many of you remember this popular dance venue? Anyway, there was a yard brother who classed himself as a deejay called Superstar but many knew him as **Spade,** a notorious con artist. Day and night Spade begged me to come and play at his dance, and after some weeks I relented and cancelled the dance at Roxy in favour of his. That proved to be a wrong move, and this was the part that hurt me the most. The dance was a road block, a huge success, with Barrington Levy on stage and us playing along with Frontline sound. After our sound finished beating up Frontline sound, I went to collect my money, only to find out that Spade was on his way to Heathrow Airport! I did not see him from that day until many years later. I just looked at him and slowly shook my head; he was engaged in a struggle doing mini-cabbing. He and others over the years tried their stunts and I have seen all of them end up with nothing.

One of the legendary clashes in my Soferno B days

Chapter 5

THE BIRTH OF STEREOGRAPH OUTERNATIONAL

At this particular time I was now living on the Angell Town Estate, which was to become notorious for all the wrong reasons. When my Mother got the flat at number 83 Marston House we were the third set of family to move on the estate, which was not even fully finished, so again you see I am an original Brixtonian.

Life on Angell Town Estate became such that to be safe you had to run things and have 'street cred' and be respected. I had all of these things but don't misunderstand me, I wasn't a gangster in the normal way but because of my character and associates I ran things on my turf in those times. You are loved by both young and the old you don't have to be killing and terrorising people to gain respect; you just have to know how to 'flex' with people.

I knew and moved with some real gangsters but I did not do what they did, nevertheless, they had my back covered so no one really brought their crap to my front door. In addition, I was one of the nicest brothers to know; always helping people, and many loved that. Most significantly, though, **The Good Lord** was training me for his calling later on in my life. But of course, again, I did not know this at the time. I had reflected several times on the disrespectful treatment both Neville and I had received from Soferno-B. However, I came to the conclusion that he did me a great favour for he caused my determination to soar to another level. As a result, one day I approached Neville and said to him, "Neville, is a long time I have been playing B's sound, I think is time I have my own now, and since me and you are like blood brothers, come we build a sound and take the place like a storm." To convince him further, I reminded him, "I have the experience and the knowhow, plus we are blessed because I have my own club to put the sound in - what more could we want?" I informed him that our next move was crucial for we could not let anyone know what our plan was so we had to continue as normal till we had everything in place.

Our first major decision was which technician we were going to approach to build our power amps and pre-amp, known in today's terms as a mixer, because we had to come with something different as well as having sound quality second to none. The sound I was playing at this time, Soferno-B, had a reputation for a clean and crisp (great quality) sound reproduction so we had to take it to a higher level than that to be competitive.

When you are a top class sound man you get to know a lot of people in the business and if you are well liked you will get favoured more than others. I use go regularly to Peckings Record shop at Askew Road, Shepherd Bush. He was the main UK distributor for Studio One music in the UK, and I am talking about the legendry **Coxsone Dodd** productions from Jamaica. Mr Peckings knew his music, especially the Studio One productions and no matter what selection you were playing as a sound if you are not playing certain Studio One tunes, you weren't playing. Many of the current tunes which are being played today still originate from Studio One rhythms.

Daddy Peckings had three sons, all of whom I got along with. But there was one in particular that I forged a special relationship with and that was Duke. He used to give me exclusive cuts, not only Studio One music but many others, for he had many contacts and would arrange access for me to cut the dub plates. Countless times when clashing with my many rivals some of theses same dubs Duke gave me would destroy certain sounds like Shaka, Coxsone, Saxon, and many more.

One day Duke and I were talking and I told him of my intention to leave Soferno-B but he had to keep it under cover. He asked me who I was thinking to use to build the power amps and pre-amp. In those days we did not buy factory assembled power amps; the norm was to find a technician who was turning out credible equipment. There were several at that time who were of the standard of Errol who built for Coxsone, King Tubby's, and even Quaker City sound from Birmingham, all of which sounded good. But I was looking to take things to another level. Soferno-B's technician was great but to go to him was out of the question, plus his equipment had become dated. His name was Mr. Jackson.

So Duke said to me, "I know a wicked technician whose equipment is going to mash up the place, but he has not got the big break so he does not have the street cred as yet. But trust me, Big Youth, let this brother build your amps and pre-amp and you won't regret it. He has also invented this futuristic effects called a **Bi-Phaser** and I know you know quality when you hear it so let me arrange a meeting with him and you can tell him what you want."

Because I respected Duke's opinion I spoke with Neville and showed him what Duke had told me. We decided to meet this technician, whose name was **Winston** and his equipment was called Troggs Electronic. We made arrangements to meet up at his home in some high rise block of flats along the Chelsea embankment, just before you reach Earls Court.

I will never forget that Monday afternoon. Winston was a slim, brown skin, Black British brother and very eccentric in his behaviour. But what a genius! This is why one should never judge a book by its cover. Duke introduced us to him and there was an instant connection.

I started to outline our requirements and I explained that this equipment would have to be second to none for I had my reputation to think as one man who was proud of my status in the sound world. He was very confident he could supply me with what I wanted and we considered that my use of his equipment would catapult him into nationwide recognition.

Winston himself was involved with his own sound system which he called **Alpha** and on which he played, obviously using his own equipment. He was therefore enthusiastic in suggesting for me and Neville to come and listen to it to get a first-hand experience of his equipment. They were playing out the following week and we went to hear it. The quality was already superb, but what we did not know was that by divine inspiration, he would end up building our sound better than his.

Winston said, "I am going to give you a secret weapon to destroy your rivals – it's called a **Bi-Phaser** and I will make your **pre-amp (mixer) with parametric equalisation**." Now this type of equalisation was not being used by any other sounds at that time because, for one: the cost; and two: this type of quality was only used in the expensive professional recording studios.

With a feeling of mutual benefit and within a feeling of great vibes, we got down to business straight away, arranging the manufacture of my sound equipment. The Bi–Phase pre-amp (mixer) was awesome, not to say that there were not other phasers on the market but there were no sounds using them and, most of all, this custom built one was in a class of its own.

With this in motion we needed to build boxes but also to consider when the time came to leave Soferno-B, who was going to move with us and who we would have to leave behind, based on who are our dedicated and trustworthy friends. There were a few for whom my decision to leave them behind was not a tough one. There were those who wanted my position as top dog from a long time so they were not going to break away with me, and there was one in particular who at that time I wanted to dispose of him because he had done the lowest of things any man could do to someone who brought him up from nothing.

I am speaking of the one **Barabus** (which is not his real name, because many of you know him and if I exposed his real name he would certainly lose any little ratings that he may have, and that is not my aim). Anyhow, there are some of you who will work it out. Barabus was on Soferno-B sound with me and he robbed me for over a year and half, twice a week totalling grands. Yet I was the one who took him in as my apprentice and taught him how to select sound. The trust I had in him meant he was collecting the money at my club-door every Thursday and Sunday nights. Being too trusting I did not count the money when he came up with security. I just paid my staff and my other expenses; what ever total he told he had taken I believed him. What a fool I was.

One day another member of my crew knew what was going on and felt so bad that he could not keep it anymore, especially because he knew how well I treated all my workers. He came to me and said, "Big Youth, you pay this boy - he works for you; how comes he wearing so much expensive crocodile shoes, all the latest designer garments, his girlfriend got fur coats plus top of the range handbags." Now this was all he said to me and walked away. My brain now was going at a hundred miles per hour - what did he mean by this? For days I was wrestling with what he had said to me and then it came into my mind ... "But you never check your takings from the door? But no, this boy could never be mad enough to be robbing me, him must want to die."

I remember it like yesterday. It was Sunday night and this boy came up as normal, placed the takings on my office desk, told me a total and started to make his way out of the office like he normally would. I then said to him, "Hold a minute. How much did you say is there?" He told me some figure and this was where the confirmation was going to be had that he was robbing me. I told him to count it. By this time sweat is pouring out of his forehead like a river. I am just staring into his eyes. You could feel the tension. The amount he told was short by £150. I said, "Count it again." By this time I wanted to do him something terrible. What this crook was doing was that twice a week, depending on how much takings there was, he would pocket a certain amount. Now imagine, over the space of time, 18 months, how much this snake had pocket from me.

My security staff and some of the sound crew wanted to dispose of him but I was going to introduce him to justice. He was lucky that one main reason why we did not take him for a drive was that his mother and my Father were long time friends it was his mother who had begged me to take him amongst me as he was getting himself into all kinds of trouble with police. Well, again, you know the old saying, **Sorry fi marga dog it turn round bite you** (showing compassion for someone only for that person to show no gratitude).

He wangled his way back into Soferno-B after I had left because he too had always wanted my position. Even to this day he is going around playing in revival dances as Soferno-B. What a joke. And let me give you an even sweeter joke. The money he robbed from me he used it to maintain this hot girl named Carol, a really sexy looking girl. She spent all of the money he robbed from me and then one of my villain friends from the Raiders crew, who used to run Brixton for a time, took her away from him and he could not do anything about it.

This individual, who I call Barabus, even has the nerve to be telling those who are willing to listen that the reason I put him to collect the money at the door of Bali-Hi was that I felt threatened by his ability as a selector. Let me again set the record straight: this person could hardly be called a top class selector; he has never played in a top class clash and defeated anyone. Furthermore, like many other of these hyped up selectors, he cannot take the microphone and say his name let alone address and entertain dance fans. This is another of what I call "jukebox selectors"; push the button and they put the record on. The statements he is making is to try and take away the shame of what he had done to me but that is something he will have to live with or make amends for.

In my life I have had so many different experiences, fit enough to aid me in gaining a wise mind, knowledge, and understanding. However, when two close friends of mine committed suicide, that was something I could never understand then, but it showed me how fragile man can be.

So now I had sorted out whom my team would be, my next step was to build some speaker boxes and inform certain co-members of Soferno-B about my intention for my new team. Neville and I were planning everything to a tee. At this time, Villa Road was our HQ and this is exactly where we were going to start to build some of the speaker boxes; some were made by ourselves and others were ordered. These included the famous box called **Paul Bogle** as Stereograph boxes were named after Jamaican National Heroes or other things we associated with our culture, like Rizla, which was one of the top end boxes. There's no need to guess where that name came from because in those days I was one of the biggest herbal smokers – yes, high grade ganja. This may shock some of you reading this book who might only have known me in these latter days. You are in for more shocks because the truth has to be spoken.

We started to gather the rest of equipment which would be needed, such as cables, etc. Everything had to be to the highest specification for maximum quality as a priority. Winston advised us that as long as we didn't try to cut corners by buying sub standard accessories then everything would be fine, and so we proceeded in accordance with his advice.

Stereograph set the trend in using a concrete slab to seat the turntables on, instead of the usual piece of sponge, in order to minimise vibration and improve sound quality. After this, most sounds started to use a concrete slab thinking that this would make them sound better like Stereograph, and the ones who did not try it was because they did not want to be seen to be following Stereograph. That's how it goes when you are a trend setter.

It took us 7 days non stop work to finish the boxes we were making for ourselves. The reason we had to move fast was because we were going to drop the bombshell on Soferno-B the Monday night and Stereograph would have to be ready to play in the place of the out going Soferno-B for the Sunday night session at **Bali-Hi. We** could let JAH SHAKA play on his own on the Thursday night but we would have to be ready for the Sunday.

The reason I named the sound system **Stereograph** was because 'stereo' represented the sound it would produce, and 'graph' for the obvious graft or hard work which had been put and would be maintained in the sound. Now, many thought that I took the name from Daddy U-Roy's sound, which was in Jamaica, but if they knew the correct spelling and pronunciation they would have known that they were both different. His sound was spelt **Stur-Gav** but because of how many of us pronounce things they sounded the same. So that's another issue cleared up.

Now, after everything was in place it was time for me and Neville to go and inform SOFERNO-B of our move. I will never forget it. I removed all the equipment which I had purchased over the years with my monies; because of my love for the sound, it was nothing for me to purchase certain things without being reimbursed. I did not take even a pin which he had bought because I did not want him saying that I took his equipment to build my sound, but because his mind was on other things, such as the record shop, he had not realized the amount of equipment I had purchased over the years.

Bali-Hi Club – Chabba and Silver Fox

And the very comment which I was trying to avoid is exactly what I was told by numerous people that he had said. Mind you, I should have expected this because his sound was about to go into oblivion. The sound truck used to be parked at my house with the equipment. However, on this occasion I drove it to his house and pulled up outside his gate with feelings of mixed emotions, even though I intended to enjoy every second of what was about to unfold. Neville also pulled up outside his gate driving his car. I rang his door bell with the pre-amp in one hand and the keys for his truck in the other. After a few seconds he opened the door with is usual smug smile. "What happen, Big Youth! My reply was, "From this day, I no longer will be playing your sound. I have taken everything which was purchased with my monies and I have not touched so much as a pin which belongs to you and also, as from today, your sound will no longer be playing in Bali-Hi." The smug smile disappeared and was replaced by an expression of utter disbelief. "And by the way," I continued, "both me and Neville need to get the monies owing to us from the record shop." I handed him his keys and pre-amp and turned around as I concluded, "This little boy you grew is no longer a boy; man ah big man." He just stood there for few seconds in shock before closing his door.

Now with that out the way, it was time to get down to some serious business. Well, as you can imagine, the haters who were left behind with him tried to make it work, but the heartbeat had just left so they were fighting a losing battle and soon had to park up and watch the ride.

One night the reduced Soferno-B were playing over at **Cubies** in Dalston and me and Neville went to listen. We could not believe the great Soferno-B sounded so terrible and their so-called selector, the one who robbed me, did not have a clue. We just walked out after a short while and laughed. Indeed, every unfair game plays twice. And by the way, for the record, Neither myself nor Neville got the money we should have received from Soferno-B from the takeover proposal - only a measly down payment not even worth mentioning. Once again, because of my kindness I have been robbed.

The Sunday was here, March 1980 and **Stereograph** was playing for the first time. The original crew, in addition to myself, consisted of **Neville** (aka, The Overseer) and co-owner, **Big D, Fitzy, Central,**

Ossie, Dego Ranks, Silver Fox, Spinner, Slang, and **Lascell** the truck driver. Later on **Marshal Lee** and **Marie Poser** joined the crew. We got there early, armed with a brand new sound and our new technician in attendance to make sure all was well. We began the sound check with the top end. It sounded so crystal clear we never heard anything so crisp before. Then the bass line... wow! The sound was shaking Bali-Hi to the rafters. The doors were then opened now and the punters started to come in. They could not believe what they were seeing and hearing. Within no time Bali-Hi was full and the dancehall fans are blown away by it all. All I could hear were great comments such as, "This sound ah boss sound," "Boy, Stereograph bad." Then I introduced them to the secret weapon. That was the icing on the cake - they never heard anything like it before... a new champion sound was born.

It was not long before my rivals were feeling threatened and the knives were out from many different angles. I had some good local talent with my sound for by now my emphasis leant towards having some good deejays who would ply their skills on the mike. We had Dego Ranks, Marshall Lee, Marie Poser, and Silver Fox. I was not too bad myself and could hype the crowd. There were also deejays like Ricky Ranking who, even though he was not fully on Stereograph, would always come and jam with us, so he was like one of us. Here comes another major talking point, which needs to be cleared up. It concerns the rivalry between Stereograph and, you guessed it, **Saxon.** Now, truthfully speaking, Saxon sound was a sound I had respect for because other youths like myself at that time were impressed by their persistence in making it and, as many know, they did not flinch from spending on their sound. But boy is boy and big man is big man.

IT'S THE STEPPING OUT SHOW!
A CULTRUAL PROMOTION
JEFF AND PRU INVITE YOU TO

A Night of
Entertainment

at

THE RIVERDALE HALL
THE LEWISHAM CENTRE
RENNELL STREET   LEWISHAM   S.E.13.

on

FRIDAY 10th SEPTEMBER 1982
FROM 8pm TILL 2am

INTRODUCING   ☆   LIVE ON STAGE   ☆
THE TOP REGGAE BAND

★ **SHEER GOLD** ★

DANCING TO —

★ **STEREOGRAPH** ★

ALSO

★ **SAXON** ★
☆ **INTERNATIONAL** ☆

TICKET IN ADVANCE £3 - 50

ADMISSION   £4 - OO   AT THE DOOR

TICKETS AVAILABLE FROM: JEFF 699 3821
AND 291 3681

The clash with Saxone, when they took full advantage of a rare technical fault which prevented Stereograph from playing that night. But this was the signing of the execution warrant which Stereograph later enforced on Saxone

Stereograph is the only sound that made Saxon to have to completely rebuild his sound after we destroyed them one night in a club called **Balham 200**. That was the lesson I felt necessary to teach him and the rest out there - don't mess with Stereograph. Previous to that night, however, my step-brother, Copper, had kept a dance with me and Saxon at a hall in the Lewisham shopping centre. Now, on that night something which rarely happened to Stereograph occurred. We had a technical fault with our pre-amp and could not play for the whole night. We tried to fix the problem, which was only a minor one, but we could not locate it at the time and Muscle Head and his crew took full advantage. I was so embarrassed and mad that if you had cut me, not one drop of blood would have come out. He had a fiesty deejay called Papa Levi, who was good, but nevertheless, how dare they disrespect Stereograph when it was me who had inspired them and I was a veteran in the business, compared to them. The worst part of it all was that their sound quality was no way in the class of Stereograph.

Muscle Head had not realized what he had done, which was to build his own coffin for his demise a few months after feeling so sweet about the Lewisham incident. He accepted a date to play with me again but this was to prove to be the biggest mistake Saxon would make. This session at Balham 200 was to become my revenge session. Both sounds set up and, as usual, Muscle Head started to run off his mouth. What he did not realize was that I was not ready to turn up the heat until the dance was full. When dance was in full swing it was time for Saxon to be vanquished. I used him like a punch bag – a little mid-range jab here, a flurry of top-range jabs, and then a killer bass across his jaw. Even when he dropped I picked him up and started pounding him again. My bass line shook every nut and bolt out of his sound. Remember I told you about Marshall Lee? Well, he was an on-fire young Jamaican deejay who was on form that night. He made Saxon's Papa Levi look totally ridiculous. At that time they even had Maxi Priest who used to sing on their sound but that could not save Saxon sound from dying that night. It got so embarrassing that Muscle Head had to turn off his sound. How dare they test us.

A couple of days later I went to see Winston, our technician, for him to do our regular service but there was something strange about his behaviour, it was not normal. Now let me explain, I was Winston's main asset because from when he built for Stereograph his ratings went sky high and he became the most sought after technician. Henceforth, whenever I went to his house I had free roam. However, on this occasion he did not want me to go into his workroom, which was strange. But see how the God I serve is awesome. By some unknown force the workroom door just opened mysteriously, and guess who was hiding behind it... none other than the owners of Saxon - Muscle Head and Dennis Rowe. They wanted to just disappear but I just looked at them and shook my head. Winston did not know what to say.

So there it was, the great Saxon had thrown away all of his sound equipment just as how one would throw away rubbish, and came to my technician for him to build them a completely new sound with the expectation and requirement that it must be at lest equal to Stereograph or better. To ensure this, he let Winston know that money was not a problem. Finally, Saxon got his new sound, but to his frustration it still could not sound like Stereograph, which brought Muscle Head and Winston in constant disputes. After a time, Saxon went and built another sound with different equipment in his bid to outdo Stereograph. That made it the second sound that Saxon had to abandon in pursuit of the higher standard and quality of Stereograph. As they say, "Don ah don, and Donovan ah Donovan". Let me reveal some more unknown truths about how Muscle Head and Dennis Rowe tried to put a stop to Stereograph in more ways than one, only to create a whip for their own backs.

As expected, there were certain producers or music agents who would sell dubs to the big sounds so most of us were quite acquainted with the suppliers of each other.

I was a close friend of a producer called Robert Livingstone who, in those days, used to control all of Bunny Wailers' production from his Solomonic label and in later times became manager to major recording artist, Shaggy. Robert would let me cut anything I wanted. He would also sell Saxon and others a few tunes. Listen to this, Saxon offered Robert cash and jewellery if he would not give certain dubs to me but deal with them exclusively. In other words, they were trying to price me and other sounds out of the running. What they did not realize was the respect Robert had for me, so he came to me laughing and said, "What is wrong with those people, don't they know that you are my close friend and I have respect for you?" So I replied, "Robert, let them have a few dubs and make some money from them." But I knew all the tunes that they were given and they could not get certain dubs that I got. They had just made a whip for their backs because the word would soon spread that Saxon is paying over the odds for tunes so everyone they dealt with would up their prices. This made it hard for some sounds to afford dubs because as far as the producers were now concerned, if Saxon could pay those prices so can the rest. Muscle Head and Dennis Rowe will never admit this because until now I have never confronted them about it and as far as I know, I am the only selector who can say this for it was not something I heard but actually can prove it.

I was never one for giving interviews. I have only done one interview, which was with Paddy from Studio One sound on Lightning Radio and I made one guest appearance on a radio show on Roots FM with Duke Peckings. I have never made any of those clips you now see on YouTube with some self-confessed so-called veterans in the sound business who claim to know everything. I have just kept quite and let them talk. Some of the things they say are true but there is so much that has not been revealed because they simply do not know it. The other factor is also that if the truth be spoken it would take the gloss off their stories, exposing them as being not all they claim to be. That is why some are going to hate this book because it has revealed certain hidden truths and there are others who are going to love it because they longed for certain truths to be revealed, while others will now know who did what and who deserve respect and credit. **The truth often hurts**.

Many years later I was at a dance where Saxon was playing with **Luv Injection** and **V-Rocket**. Muscle Head came to me and said, "Most respect to you; as much as my sound is firing it still cannot sound like Stereograph." I respect Muscle Head for that, even though it was many years later that he spoke the truth. So now you know the truth about Stereograph and Saxon. I still have to say this again, I have maximum respect for Saxon's Muscle Head for he is still playing, which I am not. But just like me, he gets a big fight from certain other soundman who can't stand to see sounds like Stereograph and Saxon who came and made their impact on the sound business. They act as if they are the only ones who have done anything in the business, and you know what the biggest joke is? These so-called top men have never owned their own sound. And on the odd occasion if they did, it was not even worth mentioning. So how on earth can these men come and disrespect a man like me or Muscle Head? Out of order. This is why I just ignore them when they are talking a loud of rubbish. So big up yourself Muscle Head, and don't worry, Chabba is not bringing back Stereograph (smile). One of the reasons I have included the chapters about my sound days in my book is because it was a special time in my life. Also, there are many who would like to know the truth and the truth must be spoken. It would have been a shame if it was not told and I did not share it with you all.

Chapter 6

TIME TO LEAVE ENGLAND

It was now the start of the 80s, at which time I began to show signs of **an illness** which, although I did not realise it at the time, would plague me to this very day. Had it not been for the mercy of God and His calling on my life, I certainly would not be here today to write this book. Thank you, Jesus.

There was a terrible numbness and pain in the left side of my body, from the top of my head down the whole of my left side. On further medical investigation they were still not quite sure what it was. In those days they did not have the sophisticated medical equipment they have now, so they gave what was called a *lumbar punch* to get some fluid from my spine to see if they could diagnose the problem, which they knew was spinal. The doctors assumed that I had a cyst pressing on a nerve in my spine, causing this numbness. They wanted to do an experimental operation. The problem was that this could well have left me crippled, so obviously I refused. Even though I was in pain, I was young and still enjoying myself; I felt I could cope regardless of the discomfort. I did not know that this illness was going to be with me all my life and have drastic consequences.

Here comes another turning point on the social scene, which was also another turning point in my life. It was April 1981 and Bali-Hi was still in full swing. We were just about to keep a big bank holiday dance when all hell broke loose. The **Brixton Riots** exploded. As I had previously stated, the relationship between the Black community of Brixton and the police was never good. A lot of damage was done over the years by the government enforcing the dreaded SUS laws. This enabled the police, without any substantial evidence, to stop and search or arrest anyone who they thought or suspected had or was going to commit a crime. No need to say, the majority of police officers used this at their will, out of racism, to harass the Black youths of Brixton. As a result, morale was at an all time low and it was just a matter of time before the crap would hit the fan.

It was Friday evening 10th of April, 1981 when a Black youth got stabbed. Now, instead of the police assisting the injured youth they were more concerned with arresting people, which did not go down well with the bystanders. Within a flash it was off; the Brixton community said enough is enough and turned on the police. It started in Railton Road but soon spread like wild fire.

By the Saturday it was now a full scale war. In all the years I had lived in Brixton I had never seen anything like this – police cars overturned and on fire, shops being burned and looted, and an all out physical attack on the police officers who were being injured left, right and centre. Paradoxically, I can remember seeing one of the funniest scenes I have ever witnessed in my life. Right on the corner of Atlantic Road and Brixton Road, where Foot Locker store is now situated, was the site of a men's clothes shop called Burtons. The rioters had just smashed the window and one of the looters was running down the road with a fully dressed display dummy which he had grabbed, no time to undress it.

Of course, many in the community were genuinely rebelling and fighting for the cause, but you know there were those who were seizing the opportunity to ply their trade – theft. However, while those opportunist Black youths were looting the small stuff, the big villain White men came with removal vans and cleaned out entire stores while the aggrieved Blacks were busy fighting the police for their rights. Sounds familiar? Same old story. Brixton town had taken on a complete different appearance. It was a full scale war zone. The police were driving around like packs of wild dogs picking off any isolated Black youths they could get and giving them a beating before reaching the station with them. Others were engaged in running battles with youths armed with bricks, bottles, and Molotov cocktails – the first time they were used in mainland Britain, which helped to reduce the environment to a raging inferno.

It was about 6.30 in the evening when my telephone rang (my house phone, that is, as there were no mobiles then) and a voice said, "Hello, is that you Michael?" It was Phil, the manager for Bali-Hi. He continued, "I've just spoken to the police chief on the phone and he wants an urgent meeting with you at the club. Can you get here in the next hour?" This was not sounding good. I jumped into my car and made my way to the club. When I got there the police chief was already present with two other officers. He stated his business.

"We know that you run this night club on Thursday and Sunday nights with anything between seven hundred to one thousand clubbers and you carry a fair influence in the community." I was eager to know what his business there was. He continued, "In the light of what has been happening, we will have to close you down until further notice." What did they think that I was, stupid? I knew that there would be no 'further notice'. These spiteful police officers used the Brixton uprising as a convenient excuse to shut me down. There were certain officers who knew I ran Bali-Hi and did not like how I as a young Black man was driving the latest cars. But I was no criminal, no drug dealer or pimp, therefore there was nothing they could do to me – my business was legitimate, so they always bore a grudge. They had now finally gotten their hearts desire. The great Bali-Hi was being closed down and with it the end of a wonderful era. The whole music fraternity was stunned, but it was now time for me to move on, they cannot keep a good man down.

A lot of people think that the use of the hardcore drug called crack-cocaine only surfaced in the 'hood' in the early nineties. Well, some of the gangsters I knew were taking crack from as early as 1972; they just kept it under cover as much as they could, including one of my big brothers, who was a top dog in those days. This nasty, evil, Satan drug was to eventually claim my brother's life. He has been missing since 1985, with no trace of him to this time. Although I have no substantial proof of this, I am convinced in my heart that he has been wiped out by the drugs underworld. So you see, I have a first-hand experience of what heartache cocaine can cause. To this very day my whole Family is still grieving.

One of the many things that I am thankful to God for is that I had enough common sense and willpower not to even think of trying Class A drugs. My only involvement with drugs, then, was that I smoked the high grade weed, and that was good enough for me. I had many friends who said they would never try it but they all ended up taking cocaine, resulting in some serious consequences.

Now with my club closed and having done pretty much everything in the sound system business in England, it was time to pursue another goal in my life. As I told you, I was born in Brixton but my parents came from Jamaica, which I had always wanted to visit and to know. Now, however, I had an added motive; I wanted to go and conqueror the sound business out there, which was a tall challenge.

At this time my step-brother, Copper, who I told you kept the dance with me and Saxon, was intending to return home to Jamaica to live. Because of his love for music and what he had seen me achieve in the business, he wanted to build up a sound system on his return there. But there were a couple of significant factors for him to consider beforehand. Firstly, he had no experience in the sound business, and secondly, he didn't know what equipment he would need. After several months of discussion he realized that he would have to have someone like me to achieve his aim, so I thought to myself that as we are Family, we could do it as a joint venture and make it a reality. I introduced him to my technician Winston, who had built Stereograph, and we ordered some power amps, a mixer, and you know what, yes, a Bi-Phaser. If we were going to take Jamaica by storm we would have to come good.

The speaker cabinets would be built out there but we would ship over readymade speakers and all other necessary equipment. It looked like finally I was going to go to Jamaica, but not for a holiday; I was going to live there and say goodbye to England.

I talked it over with Neville and although he was sad to know this was my intention, he gave me his blessing. Now here is another point of talking that needs to be cleared up. Many people thought that I took Stereograph equipment to build this new sound in Jamaica, but no, not one piece of Stereograph equipment went with me. This was a different venture. It was also my and Neville's intention that Stereograph would continue to play with my then existing crew still running it. It would have been unfair of me not to leave it running, for apart from the financial input, which was always down to me and Neville, they had also put in their hard work into Stereograph.

Copper was ready to fly out before me and he would come to meet me at the airport when my time arrived. Everything was going to plan and the time was fast approaching when I would be leaving. Coincidentally, just before I left for Jamaica, I received an offer from the housing department of my own first accommodation, a flat (apartment), guess where? On **Somerleyton Road, in Southwyck House** (the newly built 'Barrier Block'), in the exact area where I started life as a young boy. Now as young man I had gotten a two-bedroom flat there, but as events would have it, I would not be there to enjoy it. The offer came at that time as if to present me with a choice – Ja, or my own flat in UK. Well, I chose Jamaica. As time drew nearer a lot of mixed emotions came at me from various angles. Firstly, I considered that my dear old Mother would miss me like nothing. She had always been used to me being there. Then there was my girlfriend; how would I tell her that I am going away, not knowing when and if I would be back. And what of my beloved crew whom I had always flexed with? One thing was for sure, though. My sound rivals would be glad to see the back of me. I was sure they couldn't wait to try and take liberties with Stereograph in my absence.

Now listen to this, if this is not pure balls. I bought a one way ticket because I was planning on a long stay with the intention of achieving my goal, which was to have a champion sound and a top class production label in the capital of reggae music. Despite the hype that certain other selectors and soundman loved to generate, they had never attempted, let alone, achieved what I did. By now my name was no longer Big Youth, it was now **Chabba Melo** – gwaan, my youth!

The time had finally arrived. I was leaving England the next day, **Sunday the 15th May, 1983**. The Stereograph crew kept a going away party for me on Railton Road. Now listen to this drama. We used to play sessions at a venue called **The Factory Club** at Chippenham Mews, off the Harrow Road and, talk about fatal attraction, a young female who always used to attend fell head over heels in love with me. The weird thing about this was that I never knew what she looked like. I only ever spoke to her over the phone after she got her brother to pretend to be a dance promoter and obtained my telephone number that way. After many months, curiosity got the better of me and I decided to meet her the night before I am to fly to Jamaica. A fatal mistake. I arranged to meet her at Brixton tube station but because I had to check so many people and also to attend my going away party, I completely forgot. Anyway, after a long period of waiting she decided to ring my house phone and my Mum kindly let her know, "I don't why he arrange to meet you knowing fully well he is going away tomorrow."

You can imagine, this girl was gutted. Her name was Ann and my Mother told me that after I left she would ring constantly wanting to know when I was coming back. My Mother said she was cool at first, always polite, but after a few months she turned nasty and I mean, nasty. She threatened to burn down my Mum's house and all kinds of abusive talk. She told my Mum she hoped they hang me by my balls in Jamaica.

My younger brother could not take her constant abuse of my Mum anymore and decided to take her on. She told him in no uncertain terms that she was going to get some men from over her side to waste him. My Mother had to change the house number to finally get rid of her. Do you still want to be a top class selector?!

Sunday 15th May, 1983 had finally arrived and it was time to go to the airport. But the dramas never stopped with me. I was booked to travel on a well known airline at that time, one which flew regularly to Jamaica, called **Air Florida**. Hear this now. The same day I am to fly out they went bust! They had to re-route passengers, so instead of a non-stop flight to Kingston, I ended up at Washington DC in America. On reaching there, I found that the airline had arranged transfer and hotel accommodations because we would have to stay overnight. But the drama continued. First of all, as soap powder was in short supply in Jamaica at that time, I made sure I was well prepared by carrying one pillow case full of it. When I got to customs at Washington I only heard a voice behind me say in a deep American accent, "What's this you got here? It looks like cocaine." I had to laugh for I knew it was soap powder but this big officer didn't. He said, "Come with me." After testing it and finding out that it was soap powder, they said I was free to go, but then came more drama.

I met this guy on the plane and being social we started a conversation. Boy, this guy could talk! Now, both of us were going to be staying at the same hotel overnight and we were to share a taxi together. As we got outside the airport terminal, I saw this car drive up with three dodgy looking fellows. They gave me the once over glance and then drove off. Now this chatterbox brother was too busy talking to observe these guys. Shortly afterwards, these two hot looking girls approached me and started giving me compliments about a massive ghetto blaster which I was carrying. They then asked me if we could watch their car while they go to collect someone because they did not want to get a parking violation.

Within a short space of time they returned without the person they were supposed to be meeting and offered to drive us to the hotel where we would be staying. Mr Chatterbox was ready to go with them, thinking he had pulled, but what they did not know was that I was street wise and knew that this was a ploy to rob us. They were working with those guys who drove by earlier and clocked me. If we had gone with them I would never have reached Jamaica. Later I told this to the taxi driver who took us to the hotel and he said I was "one lucky son of a bitch", that if I had gone with them they would have "robbed and smoked" me – yes, gun shot.

And the saga went on. By now, because of the diversion of my flight, I was a day late arriving in Jamaica. My step-brother and some of my cousins (who I had never met, but who were supposed to pick me up) were not outside waiting for me as I'd expected. Can you imagine, I didn't know where I was going, and the Jamaican heat was like I had walked into a furnace. Hustlers were toting left, right and centre, either offering taxi service or wanting to buy English or American currency.

I could not afford for them to realize that this was my first visit or that I am not a born and bred Jamaican, so time to test my patwa (authentic Jamaican speaking which I had perfected to a tee over the years! YU AH HEAR ME (Are you hearing me)? MAN JUST LOW ME AND GWAAN WHEY YU AH GO (Just leave me alone and go to wherever it is you are going). I heard one of them say to the other, "Yu no know Yard man wen yu see them?" (Do you not know a Jamaican when you see one?). I said in my mind: 'Yes, Chabba, you have this under control.' After a little search I found my brother and cousins drinking in a bar.

I chastised them, "Look how long me deh yah a search fi yu. Copper, whey you ah deal wid, have man outside like fool?" (Look how long I have been searching for you, what do you think you are doing letting me wait outside as if I am a fool?). My two cousins looked stunned. They could not believe what they were hearing – this can't be a man who was not born in Jamaica, coming here for the first time and speaking like this. One of them said, "Tell me something, is the first time you are coming to Jamaica?" I replied, "Yes!" He smiled and said, "Boy, you are the real thing." We loaded up the car and set off for **Mandeville,** which is in the parish of Manchester. This was to be my new home for the next six years and the start of another chapter in my life. What was going to happen again was beyond belief.

As we were driving I was taking in the scene and thinking to myself that I have finally arrived. Many things were just as how I had pictured them, and some were completely new. Now most Jamaican men love a drink, so about half way through the journey we stopped at a bar my cousins were familiar with. There was this sweet looking brown skin girl serving behind the bar. "Jackie!" One of them shouted. "Give us three hot Heineken," (meaning not taken from the fridge) then he turned to me and asked, "What you want to drink, Chabba?" I asked for a soda as I was never one to drink alcohol. They laughed, "You going have to do better than that."

The girl who was serving behind the bar was looking me over and smiling. She said to me, "You just reach in." I said yes. She said, "Hear what happen, just remember where I am, an' when you settle off just link me. I am not in no joke business." Talk about straight to the point! One of my other cousin said, "Boy, Jackie is staking her claim a'ready – gwaan, Chabba, yu big bout yah" (keep on, you are in total control). I thought to myself, these Jamaican girls are different to the English girls; they speak it how it is. My companions finished their beers and my cousin said, "Come, mek we move... Hey Jackie, don't worry, me ah go mek Chabba link you soon (Let's go, don't worry we will bring him back to see you)." A big smile lighted her face and she said to me, "Remember what I said," and we headed out.

By time we got to Mandeville it was night. It was a long drive from Norman Manley Airport in Kingston and I was on a high – not drugs but my adrenalin was flowing with the excitement of finally being in Jamaica. We pulled up outside my cousin's home, a lovely four bedroom house, built upon a hill overlooking Mandeville. What a beautiful sight. We went inside and he showed me my room. My step-brother, Copper, with whom I had planned to build the sound, had his own house but he had rented it out whilst living in England and was then waiting for the tenants to move out. So for then, we all stayed at our cousin's.

I went outside on the veranda (front porch) and gazed up into the sky. What a beautiful sight it was. I had never seen so many stars before, and some unfamiliar sounds of the insects just blew me away.

Not long after, they had prepared dinner, but I was not hungry so I drank a glass of Kool Aid punch, which had me wanting more. The main thing on my mind was to thank God for a safe journey and for his protection through this new venture in my life.

It was not very long before it was morning, but I did not really sleep through the night. Anyway, outside I heard this peculiar noise that sounded like a goat. When I looked through the window to the back of the house, indeed, tied to a tree, was a ram goat. My cousin, whose house I was staying at, is the eldest son. He said, "Yes, that goat for you. We are going to keep a welcome party for you and that goat is going to make *mannish water* and curry goat." *Mannish water* is a soup made from parts of the goat such as the head and intestines. You could not get fresher than that. Now most Yard (Jamaican) men I know do not eat the meat of a female goat; it has to be the male so that's why they use a ram goat which, by the way, is supposed to give men stamina (get the drift?).

My next introduction to Jamaica was how to cope with the heat. I had just taken a shower and by the time I walked a short distance it was if someone turned a hose pipe on me; I was soaking wet! I had to go back and take a shower again. Until I got acclimatised, the sky juice vendors could have purchased a house out of me with the amount of money I spent, constantly drinking this ice-cold refreshment, which is shaved ice with syrup and lime.

My cousins were all taxi drivers and they ran the Mandeville circuit. They had left out early for work so I got another taxi from nearby and made my way into Mandeville town centre. Even though there was similarity to Brixton, this was the real McCoy. I was used to seeing a mixture of races in Brixton but everywhere I look I saw only Black people like myself. The place was buzzing – no time wasting. The men were doing some serious hustling to survive as there is no unemployment benefit here. Life seemed to be about the survival of the "fittest of the fittest".

There was a record shop out by the square and the music was just pumping out of it. A man passing by was crying out, "Nutsey!" He was selling peanuts. Then I had my first encounter with some of the wickedest of hustlers – the "back up man dem". They literally sell you in the sense that they make their money by seeking out passengers and then loading them into the buses and the route taxis super fast. For this the drivers would then give them a percentage. Well, you can imagine, if you were not able to stand your ground they would force you into any vehicle they were loading that was going your way at the time. Another thing, you can forget about the word 'full'. It does not exist in their vocabulary for they pack you in like sardines. I looked around and smiled, and thought, "Ah yard me deh." (I am in Jamaica). My step-brother soon caught up with me. "Everything cool?" "Yeah, man," I replied.

Now my first mission was to listen to all the top sounds on the island, to suss out the opposition and see who had the best set and the greater clarity, then to make plans for the assault. Our equipment was not due to arrive until the next couple of weeks. At this time in 1983 the top sounds were **U-Roy's** sound, King **Stur-Gav** (with the selector, Inspector Willie, and deejays Charlie Chaplin, and Josey Wales, to name two); **Jah Love**; **Kilamanjaro**; **Metro Media**; **Black Star**; **Arrows**; **Black Scorpio**; and **Jack Ruby.** With the exception of Jack Ruby, the others were all town (Kingston) sounds. After listening to them, I found that even though they had top deejays and good selections, I was not that impressed with their quality, which is of primary importance as far as I was concerned. A friend of my cousin, who was a technician and knew quality, suggested that I go and listen to a sound which was based in Mandeville, called **Wah-Dat**. He said their music selection was not the hottest but when it came to quality, none of the town sounds could touch it. Additionally, this was the sound that Barry G, the famous 'bogie man' radio deejay, used whenever he was on the road.

About a week past and Wah-Dat was going to play an open air session in Mandeville town centre, so I made my way down there that Saturday evening. Walking towards the dance, from a distance I could feel and hear this round bass line and as I got closer it was crystal clear. "Yes, this is how sound fi sound," I said to my brother. We stood and listen for several hours and I decided that that was the benchmark I had to measure my sound against. My first task was to find out who built his speaker cabinets because that was the design I wanted for my sound.

After doing some investigating, we found out that a woodwork shop in Mandeville made the cabinets so straight away I was on their case and met the tradesman who built them. I told him what our intention was and the quantity we needed. He gave me some specifications to look over, and after we were both clear on what was needed, he gave me a price. Now my step-brother did not like to pay out money so he wanted to shop around. I just told him straight: if we didn't build these boxes he could forget our partnership. I would go it on my own because I was the expert in this and I knew what I wanted in order to make a great impact on the Jamaican sound system world. He saw that I was serious and agreed for that cabinet workshop to build the first set of boxes. With that settled, all we had to do was to wait for the rest of the equipment to arrive from England. The name that we would call the sound had already been decided before we got to Jamaica. It was going to be called **Destiny Outernational**. I never dreamt what impact the sound would have and the storm it was going to cause in Jamaica in a relatively short space of time. This was going to be the stuff dreams are made of and I was going to achieve what no other selector from England had attempted and succeeded in doing – to build a sound in Jamaica and make history in more ways than one.

The telephone call I was waiting for finally came. The equipment had arrived and was waiting clearance at the wharf. Well, anyone who has ever sent a barrel or shipped down a container knows that the wharf is not an easy place from which to collect one's goods waiting on the cargo ships. The hustlers will eat you alive if you don't know how to handle yourself. Everyone is in on the hustle, from the customs officers to the man who raises the barrier arm at the gate to let you out. After a series of delay tactics, designed to have you eating out of their hands, the clearance officer finally comes to assess how much import duty you should pay. Listen to this scenario involving a customs officer: "What are you doing with so much equipment? It look like you going to supply the whole island... wait, these are not second-hand, they are brand new!" He is determined to build up a case, at least in his own mind, so he continued, "I can well imagine how many pounds you pay for this, plus all these other things you have here." By now you can see his brains doing over-time to come up with a figure to charge you. "Boy, I don't know where you are going to get the money to pay for this," he says in fake sympathy. Then he tells you some ridiculously high price. You think to yourself, "He's having a laugh," but you already know the trick to get round these officers; your cousins had clued you up: put a little parcel in there with a few pairs of Clarks shoes, some trainers (sneakers) and some other goodies and let him know, "You see that parcel, it's yours – I brought this for you. Take that." He craftily opens the package, he likes what he sees and his tune changes: "Don't worry, boss, I will see what I can do for you." He goes away for about half an hour, leaving you to sweat, then returns with a more realistic figure. You agree, he takes his parcel and you get your goods.

But the hustling is not yet finished. The man who drives the fork lift to move the goods shows you that it's now his time to be dealt with. Then after him, remember the man who lifts the barrier to let you out? He wants some money too. This is how it is in Jamaica.

Chapter 7

DESTINY SOUND, UP AND RUNNING

It was time now to start assembling **Destiny Sound.** News travels fast, especially in Jamaica. Word is out in Mandeville that two brothers who come from England are building a sound and by the look of things it is going to be a force to be reckoned with. There was a man I met through my cousin and both he and his brother were technicians. One was called Potter and the other was called Crab. Both were to become technicians on Destiny Sound, especially Crab who became my main technician. Now, as much as I knew about sounds, my main talent was selecting, therefore having a good technician would free me up to concentrate on playing the sound and dealing with the studio work. It was not long before we would become a formidable team.

The evening came, and with the speakers now placed in the newly acquired boxes, we proceeded to do a sound check right in front of my cousin's house. The set sounded out of this world! Being upon the hill where my cousin lived, the sound could be heard for some distance around. Sound travels far in the Jamaican air and within virtually no time at all, my cousin's yard was full with people from the surrounding areas who had made their way up. Everyone was totally amazed and could not wait for Destiny sound to play its first dance. Apart from a few final adjustments, I was more than pleased with how it sounded, and so was my step-brother, Copper.

After a couple more weeks we organised the first dance to launch the sound. It was going to be kept locally and there was real excitement in the community, with everyone wanting to hear the new sound. Now this was to be my first dance in Jamaica but I did not even have a deejay as yet so it was going to be a test of my own ability as a deejay. I wasn't worried, however, for apart from playing the sound, I wasn't too bad at deejaying, myself. I had even recorded a couple of tracks before I left England and one was a duet with Al Campbell. Now many people always told me that I was a good deejay as well and I believe that when you are a selector you should be able to take the microphone and hype up the dance, as well. You cannot depend on the actual deejays all the time because some of them will try to flop you if you have a disagreement with them.

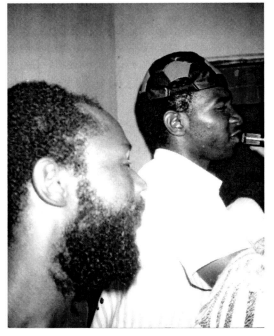

Kulcha Knox

The big day arrived and we hired a truck and took our new sound to the dance venue – a hall in Royal Flat, Mandeville. Although I was confident with much experience behind me, I was still a little nervous

– after all, I was testing myself in the capital country of my trade. But most of all, I was excited! And so was Copper. Within a short space of time the dance hall was filled with dancers who had come to hear this 'criss' new sound from England. Without an experienced crew I performed as both selector and deejay. After warming up, I got into full swing and soon had the dance in a frenzy; I was ripping it apart with repeated ovations from the crowd. We were very pleased, indeed, for Destiny had truly arrived in Jamaica. However, there is no doubt I would need a good deejay to join us as soon as possible.

Within no time, our first booking came in from a local dance promoter. We were hopeful that this dance would be a complete success as one of my other cousins said he knew this local youth who was a great deejay who was just looking for the right sound to work with and make a name for himself.

"Here is what I want you to do," I said to my cousin. "Bring him along to the next dance because I know a talented deejay or singer when I hear one. By the way, what is his name?" My cousin replied, "They call him **Kulcha Knox (Culture Knox)**."

The dance date arrived. The dance was in full operation with **Destiny** in full swing. The vibes were nice but we just needed a good deejay to make things complete. Then my cousin arrived with **Kulcha Knox** and quickly introduced him to me. He loved the vibes and the sound quality of Destiny Outernational. In fact he said he had never heard a sound with such a superior microphone input as Destiny and he could not wait to show me his talent. I 'rewind' and started the track again, then introduced him to the crowd. Straight away, as I heard him, I knew this youth had talent. And the crowd liked him, too. I knew that with his talent and humility, he could become an acclaimed top deejay within time. Well, once again I was not wrong for time was going to tell it.

Kulcha Knox had a very unique style about his delivery, and his lyrics linked the dancer with the music. Most importantly, he was confident but humble. I now had my first major deejay in place. Jamaica had not seen anything yet. This was just the start of a line of great talent that I would discover and bring to the forefront. In a short space of time Kulcha Knox and I gelled into a firm understanding with mutual respect. The word was already spreading, even though it was only our second dance, that "this sound looks like it means business."

One day I was in Mandeville chilling out in the square when a man approached me and said, "Yes, my selector. I love how you select and operate your sound. It is great." I thanked him for his compliment. This man's name was **Callo** and he was a local record producer. His family owned a bakery in Mandeville called **Collins Bakery.** Callo told me of a man named Pepe who owned a club on the Ward Avenue, uptown area. Pepe's own sound plays there with his deejay called **Bimbo**, who Callo would like me to meet. He encouraged me, "I want you to hear him, he is red hot! Very talented. Would he be the right person for you to join with Kulcha Knox and the two work together on your sound?" I decided to check out what he'd suggested.

I went up to the club one Tuesday night and it wasn't long before this slim brown youth came on the microphone: "Yes I, I man name Bimbo, watch the ride." After hearing him deliver his lyrics I knew that what Callo had told me was bang on. This youth was on fire! I went over to him and introduced myself. He acknowledged me: "Yes, respect, my boss. Callo tell me 'bout your sound and I would love to link up with you, boss." We exchanged contact details and made arrangement to link up. What I didn't know was that I was about to nurture and mentor one of the biggest reggae superstars that Jamaica would witness this century.

Another big dance promoter in Mandeville heard the sound and decided to book a date. This was a man who used the biggest of sounds in Jamaica so he knew a great sound when he heard one. The dance was a road block and **Kulcha Knox** and **Bimbo** turned it upside down! There was an instant connection between the two of them, and my step-brother was in amazement. However, what was also happening in this short space of time was that Copper himself, because of his connection with the sound, was rapidly becoming a celebrity in his own right, and slowly but surely this was going to his head. It was different for me; I was used to the limelight before I got to Jamaica. He wasn't, and eventually this was going to be his downfall and the ruination of Destiny.

Inspired by our success so far, I did not waste any time. The next mission was to start cutting (manufacturing) some dub plates, which I obtained from Kingston studios like **Channel One** on Maxfield Avenue, **Gussies** at Slipe Pen Road, **King Tubby's** and, what was to become my main dub cutting studio, **King Jammy's** over at the notorious Firehouse area (so-called because of its volatile nature, but officially called Waterhouse).

This was where I was going to forge a tight friendship with King Jammy's studio engineer, no other than **Bobby Digital,** owing to the relationship between him and me. He would give me some tunes but if Jammy's knew, all hell would have broken lose because, remember that Jammy's had his own sound and certain tracks were exclusive to him. But when you know how to treat people and they like you, all kinds of privileges will be in your favour and that was how me and Bobby Digital got on.

At this stage I have to mention my close friend, no other than the great **Sugar Minott.** He and I were tight from England and that did not change when I was there in Jamaica like it did with some other artists. He always respected what I did for him in promoting his music when he first came to England. Again Sugar was giving me the killer tracks to mash up the dances, and he had his own sound too, called **Youth Promotion**, who I later I played in a clash and gave them a proper beating. You might say how could I do this to my close bredrin, but the truth of the matter is that I had a principal where sound system was concerned. You could have been my brother, if you and I played in a clash it was dog eat dog. After the clash we were the best of friends again, no hard feelings; I just didn't like to lose, especially a sound clash.

I remember I was going to play my first clash back in England against a sound called **Jah Works**, who thought they were great. Sugar had given me a brand new track but I did not even have time to cut the dub plate for it so I played it straight from the 2-track master tape (I had a reel to reel tape machine which you would find in a recording studio). This track I am talking about was going to be a monster hit for him, later – it's called **Buy Out The Bar**. If you were a die hard dance fan you would know it. I killed Jah Works dead. He never got anymore bookings after that and another hater was added to the ever growing list.

The name **Destiny** was now spreading like wildfire all over the place, and bookings are coming in thick and fast. I was playing in a dance in an area of Manchester called **Spur Tree Hill**. I noticed a slim, tall dreadlocks Rastafarian, standing in front of the sound observing Kulcha Knox and Bimbo and giving the sound the most compliments. After a while he came up to me and said, "selector, I love how you select; I admire your performance. I am a deejay and would relish the chance to talk on your sound. My name is Tony Rebel." Well, one thing I learnt is to always give a man a chance to show what he can do. It was evident to me from the first lyric he spoke that this is a very intelligent brother. His vocabulary is wide and he has a unique delivery. He said at the end of the session that he would love to flex amongst Destiny since he did not have a regular sound to deejay on. I just said, "Yes, me bredrin, you're in."

Do see by now how God is moving in all of this. Now I had a third youth who was going to make it big in time and the numbers just continued to grow.

My cousins said they knew that Destiny was coming on fast but there was a sound in the parish of **Clarendon** called **Cosmic Force** that we would have to dispose of in order to get some major ratings. This would be the first sound with major ratings that I was going to completely destroy. They used guest deejays like the **Early B** who originated from Kilamanjaro sound, plus many more well known artists. But their main deejay was **Bunny General**, who rated himself as the best. The owner of Cosmic Force sound was a big don and he had plenty of cash so his sound was well furnished with equipment bigger in size than mine.

By this time Destiny was known by quite a few entertainers from Kingston and I knew two youths who used to be with **Black Scorpio** from Drewsland, Kingston near Marvalley. They were called **Daddy Meeky** and **Little Meeky**. However, the big deejays on **Black Scorpio** were **General Trees** and **Sassafrass**. Daddy Meeky told General Trees that he had to hear this sound from Mandeville which is taking the place by storm, so when we had the clash with Cosmic, I decided to use General Trees as my guest deejay, also a female deejay called **Lady G**. But before that, during the week leading up to the big clash, I spent time in various Kingston studios cutting fresh specials because I meant business. Cosmic sound was going to die.

The big night arrived and this was the first time General Trees was going to hear Destiny. He was blown away by it and then we got down to the business of killing off Cosmic Force. All of my entertainers were firing on all cylinders and with the barrage of music

I was playing it was not too long before Cosmic Force had to turn off his sound and let me continue playing on my own. My fans lifted me onto their shoulders, shouting out, "Chabba Melo, Destiny rule." The owner of Cosmic Force was in total disbelief but his big bad sound had just been destroyed. His name was Baller, a big thick dark man with a load of expensive jewellery around his neck. As he was walking out in disgust he gave me such a look that if looks could kill I would not be here today. Well, you guessed it – another hater had been added to the list. By the way, Cosmic sacked their selector, who was name Blacker, after this dance.

General Trees was so impressed with our performance he said, "Chabba, anytime you're playing and want me, no problem." In addition, he left with a nice fat wage packet. Now Destiny was gaining popularity at an alarming pace. My ratings as a selector had gone even higher and my personal fan base was increasing. I was spoilt for choice of girls as they all wanted to be Chabba's girl. The next revelation was about to unfold. I was playing in the same parish where Cosmic comes from, in **Clarendon**, at a place called Water Lane in Vere, because I had taken over their turf now. The dance was in full swing; Kulcha Knox, Bimbo, and Tony Rebel were taking care of the situation. Then these two bredrin came up to me. One was the singer **Patrick Andy**, who I knew, but the other one I did not know. He asked where this sound came from, sounding so good, with mike quality of such clarity. He said he had never heard such a clean sounding sound as this one and he was asking if he could sing a song on it. I said yes and I 'rewind' the tune then Kulcha Knox handed him the mike. He introduced himself, "My name is **Everton Blender**," and when he sang his song the place erupted again. He had his own unique style which was well appreciated by the crowd. He asked me afterwards if he could come and see me in Mandeville with the intention of being one of the entertainers on Destiny. I said yes and again I knew this was another star in the making. I now had three deejays and one singer, well at lest I thought so, not knowing that right there in the midst I had another world class singer waiting to be discovered.

The Kingston dance promoters were hearing about Destiny and it was not long before I got my first dance in Kingston. One of the most hardcore areas you could imagine, August Town, was where many entertainers originated from, such as, **Nitty Gritty, Tonto Ire**, and in the years to come, the famous, **Sizzla**. This was also the turf of the famous and highly rated **Black Star** sound system which recording artist **Tiger** used to perform with. Little did I know that he too would be hooked up with the Destiny mania in the near future.

I was booked to play at a dance venue called **Mama Ivy's.** This was one of the main dance venues in August Town, also the area from which legendary musicians **Steely & Clevie** originated, along with Steely's sound system, Silver Hawk. So if your sound was not saying anything you could forget about going there because town men don't take lightly to an 'idiot sound' so you had to make sure you got your act together. That night as I was playing at Mama Ivy's, who walked in but **Lloyd Coxsone** and **Briggy C** from Brixton, London. Lloyd came up to me and said, "Chabba, I am proud of you, your sound ah lick!" Briggy C gave me a high five and said, "I rate you, man, look where you are playing sound and tearing up the place." Steely commented, "I love how you sound, rude boy. You playing some great selections."

I had some friends who also lived in August Town; some lived up at Bryce Hill, some over in the dreaded **Angola**, and others on the August Town Road. It was time to get active in promoting the sound and picking up contacts. There was a dance promoter and record producer called **Dean** who lived in Firehouse (Waterhouse), near to King Jammy's. He fell in love with our sound and booked us to play at the big launch dance he was keeping in Mandeville to promote some of his young artists, such as: **Clement Ire, Banna Man, Red**

Rose, and the main one whose debut single he was promoting, a deejay called **Co-Pilot**. Again this artist was going to be one of Jamaica's all-time biggest recording artists after he'd changed his name, as you will see. In addition, I was now friends with **Chaka Demus** and he was going to be on the bill at the dance as well.

The venue for this launch was called Pimento Tree Lawn and every entertainer was hoping to steal the limelight. The town entertainers were in for a shock because the country entertainers were pressuring them, none more so than **Kulcha Knox** (Culture Knox). They had never heard anyone like him, or, indeed, Tony Rebel. Chaka was the deejay who had the biggest name out of all of the entertainers that night but he had to dig deep. Now, Chaka was never a deejay with big lyrics but his tone of voice and delivery was awesome and that's what made him a success in the deejay world.

Garnet Silk signing autograph at Wembley Hilton Hotel, London

110

Left: Dego Ranking, Middle: Garnet Silk, Right: me, Chabba

During the night I heard some good potential, apart from my regular crew, but there was one that caught my scout's ear. This was Co-Pilot. He had a unique, off-key style and also some great lyrics. As I said, it was his debut single that Dean was promoting – a 1985 track called **Heat Under Sufferer's Feet**, which used the **Pass The Kuchi** rhythm, made popular by the Mighty Diamonds and then later on by the Black British group, Musical Youth. This group got their initial recognition from Sugar Minott who had the major hit, Good Thing Going at that time and used them as support artists on his UK tour. Anyway, Co-Pilot fell in love with Destiny and said to me, "Anytime you ah play and need me, let me know." A few weeks later, I booked him to work with us at a dance in a place called Mile Gully in

111

Manchester. When he came that night we could not get him off the microphone, even at 5 o'clock in the morning! I had to turn the sound off with him still wanting to go – that's how much he was feeling Destiny. He did a few more dances with us but living in the town he sometimes found it hard to travel down so he started going round to King Jammy's studio. Jammy's saw exactly what I saw in him but the only thing he did not like was the name Co-Pilot, so **HE CHANGED HIS NAME to no other than the big Grammy winner, SHABBA RANKS.** Yes, the great Shabba Ranks, for a brief spell, was on Destiny sound. I wonder if he would remember this – you know success sometimes affect memories.

It was my intention to start recording the artists who were with the sound, thereby establishing the Destiny label. But my step-brother with whom I owned the sound was blinded by the immediate money being made so he could not see my vision. In addition, he did not like paying out money and I often had to argue with him to make sure the entertainers got paid after their work. If only he could see the gold mine which was in front of us, as long as we were fair and just.

By this time, I was about to find one of Jamaica's greatest singers. As I told you Bimbo was a deejay and a good one but on a couple of occasions in the dances he would break into a short couple of lines of singing, but never long enough for me to evaluate his full potential. One night as we played, Bimbo took the microphone and sang the old Johnny Nash classic, **I Can See Clearly Now**. My ears stood to attention. I thought to myself, Wow! This youth can sing. Henceforth, I started to encourage him to sing more on the sound, even teaching him some breathing techniques and the correct position to hold the microphone. At first he was upset, thinking I was saying that he wasn't a good deejay – but it wasn't that; I heard in him an even greater singer. Slowly but surely, he was taking my coaching and mentoring on the singing. And he began to get even better. Soon, those around could hardly believe what they were hearing, and neither could he. After a period of time I became confident he was ready to record some specials for the sound.

I told Bobby Digital, my studio engineer at King Jammy's, about Bimbo but I knew at first he thought I was just hyping up one of my entertainers. Anyway, I booked some time at Jammy's to voice some specials with Bobby and I introduced Bimbo to him: "Hello, Bobby this is my singer I have been telling you about." He looked at Bimbo and nodded his head, "Yes, my youth."

Bobby lined up the rhythm tracks while Bimbo slipped on the headphones and lined himself up in front of the microphone. He started to sing and I stood, watching the expression on Bobby's face. It was one of total amazement. In no time Bimbo voiced four specials for the sound then Bobby turned to me and said, "Chabba, I want him to voice some tracks for Jammy's." I laughed, "Yes, Bobby. You and I wi' talk 'bout that."

Subsequently, Bimbo rarely deejayed; it was mainly singing that he did and he was just getting better and better. This was the young man whom I had groomed. He and I had a big brother relationship for a long period of time; he even lived with me and we would often share one plate of food. He was such a warm and loving person. This young man was eventually to become none other than the **late great GARNETT SILK**. I had done it again. By God's divine inspiration I had found and mentored another superstar. But you know what is hurtful? A lot of men who have done less than a fraction of what I have achieved in the music business are hyping up themselves and disrespecting me. That's why I had to set the records straight and let the truth be known.

The time was now 1985 and Destiny has destroyed quite a few sounds. However, I was hunting down the big town sounds like **Kilamanjaro,** who was, at that time, the most talked about sound with the famous duo, **Early B** and **Supercat.** I had my eyes on them, bidding my time. But guess what happened. A sound from the same area as Black Scorpio (Kingston), called **GT International**, emerged on the scene and defeated the great Kilamanjaro in Skate Land at Half Way Tree, Kingston, thus becoming the new talk of the town. One of the big dons, who was also a friend of mine and a follower of Destiny, decided to put on a big dance with this new top ranking sound in town – GT versus Destiny. He wanted me to take another big scalp from town. The dance was going to be kept at the **Taurus Club, Royal Flat** in Mandeville.

Now, because of their recent success, GT were on cloud nine and thought they were invincible, that they could never be destroyed by any sound, let alone a country sound. What a fatal mistake on their behalf. They did not know who Chabba Mello or Destiny was, so while they were busy basking in their glory, I was lining up a barrage of specials, because "sound hafi dead." As Tenor Saw sang, "Ring the alarm, another sound is dying". I left no stone unturned, as usual, even going as far as to record some specials with GT's main singer **King Kong.** He did not know what was going to hit him. GT sound came from the same Kingston area as General Trees, who was close friends with the owner, a brother called **Altiman**. But by now I had a good vibes running between me and General Trees and I wanted him to be guest deejay on my sound for the night. General Trees said the only way he would do the date was if he deejayed on both sets so that there would be no ill feelings. That was fair enough, so I agreed. But what General Trees did not know was that, far as I was concerned, I would still kill GT sound and if he got caught in the crossfire, it would make no difference to me; when I was vanquishing sounds there was no room for sentiments.

At this time an old friend from Stereograph was visiting me in Jamaica, along with his baby mother and his younger brother. You are not going to believe what this boy did (I have to call him that because

114

of what he eventually did to me later on when he became a big deejay on a legal radio station). I am not going to expose his real name because this would ruin him and even though what he had done to me was terrible, I have since then become a Born Again Christian and have forgiven him. The reason I am telling this incident is to show you one of my many life threatening experiences, and to warn anyone who is in the drugs game, or thinking of entering it, that there is only one ultimate outcome – grief.

The income earned from drugs is blood money, and there is a price to pay, as this person I am telling you about was to find out some years after. Nothing you gain from drugs money ever lasts. It all disappears in time and if you are lucky you may live to tell the tale and change your ways, like I have done. I have to thank the good Lord for giving me the chance to repent of my ways. Another reason I am sharing this incident is to highlight the fact that you may be tempted for one reason of another to shed someone's blood but if at all possible, we should refrain from this and leave all judgement to God. I am going to call this sad person **Judas P**.

When he arrived in Jamaica I made him to rub shoulders with some big dons and promoted him as a big deejay from England because, as I like to speak the truth, he was quite good. Because of me, my close friend – the big don who was keeping the clash with GT – put Judas P on the bill as an official deejay, so he was there the night I destroyed GT International.

The night of the dance arrived and I could not wait to murder a town sound and gain another notch on my belt. The dancehall became full quickly. The session was soon in full flight and my crew of entertainers were on fire. After several rounds, GT was not as hot as he claimed to be and I decided it was time to go for the throat and finish off this great pretender. But then, just before the round which I planned to finish off GT, they became slightly revived by General

Trees who had just finished chatting on their mike. Yet that was not going to trouble me. I then played a specially designed burial tune by **Nitty Gritty**, and my entertainers were having a field day frustrating his entertainers. The dancehall fans started shouting, "Pack up GT, and take that rubbish back to town!"

General Trees went missing. He did not even wait to collect his pay. When I saw him several days later he said, "Boy, Chabba, yu wicked. Why yu do GT like that? I could not tek the embarisment." I just replied, "Boy, Trees, you kno how it guh." It became a major talking point – the great GT who had recently beaten Kilamanjaro was now beaten up by a country sound called **Destiny**. More ratings.

Time to expose that snake, Judas P. The big don who had kept the dance was really close to me. Those men controlled the high grade ganja exportation and he said to me, "Your boy, Judas P, me kinda like him. Yu feel we can trust him fi carry up some high grade ah England?" Well, I thought that this boy respected me and knew my situation when he came and saw the type of people I was moving with. Therefore, I thought, if we gave him some work (the high grade weed) to take back to England with him, and the main percentage from sales going to him, there was no way he was going to rob me and my boss.

My boss said to him, "Judas P, you can see that I am financially ok, so money is not a problem. Take my share of the consignment and buy me the thickest gold bracelet you can find and take the balance of profit for yourself." Well, with my own share I didn't want any bracelet so I told him to send my share to me in English pounds. We shook on it and he said, "Everything cool, Chabba." I cautioned him, "Judas P, don't try no crap and rob me, yu know, worse still, my boss because as you can see these man ah some serious brothers who don't take crap." He replied, "How could I even think of doing that? Look at the way both you and the don treat me." We fully loaded him with the highest grade and he returned to England. After a period of time when

I knew he must have sold the high grade, I didn't hear anything from him. My boss said to me, "What is your friend doing, is he trying to take me for a fool? He should have made contact with us by now. How come him nuh link me or you yet? Look like him taking me for a fool." Well, can you imagine how I felt? It was because of me why he got this chance and he had gone and done this.

I am now going to tell about a dark side of my life in Jamaica. After several more weeks and still no news from the snake, Judas P, the don called a meeting and said, "The boy Judas P, him have some family living in Marvalley, in town, we going to send in two shotter to deal with the programme." The don turned to me and said, "Chabba, is because I know you're a good and clean hearted brother why I don't brush (shoot) you. Because I know how you flex, you genuinely never believe that him was not to be trusted." I felt relieved. He continued, "Hear this anyway, you fancy a run to England? You can carry some work with you, if you want, and I am going to send a top shooter with you. Just show him where the boy Judas P live and he will do the rest, because you are too known in England to get involve."

This snake could have made me lose my life, all because of greed. But I was also saying to myself, no way if he sees me face to face can he disrespect me. Two tickets were booked, one for me and the other for a brother called Mr Pang – a nice brother but don't get on the wrong side of him. All his intention was to find Judas P and deal with the programme. Now I have seen the light, I look back at those days gone by and realize that God was sparing me for what he wanted me to do further on in my life. Thank you, JESUS.

We arrived at Heathrow fully loaded with the high grade, plus I was with an assassin coming through customs, yet I go through the 'something to declare' checkpoint and I was as cool as a cucumber. I gave the customs officer talk about my white rum which they took away from me in Jamaica and was told that I could reclaim it here. Again, by divine inspiration I had chosen the right customs officer to go to. After sympathising with me about the rum, he took up the high grade in his hands! I watched him keenly, still keeping my cool, and saw him throw it to one side before continuing his search. He picked up two more items that were fully loaded and again discarded them. I am not going to reveal in what disguise I had the high grade. The customs officer finally told me to close my case and go through. It was now only for Mr Pang to come through. He had gone to another customs officer but he was a professional and he blagged his way through and joined me outside.

We grabbed a taxi and headed for my long time bredrin, Neville with whom I had owned Stereograph. I could not stay at my Mum's as I had work on me, plus I was on a mission. Neville told me that some people had been talking all kind of things about me but you see, they could not come to Neville with any crap because he and I were always tight. He knew they were haters with all kinds of envious and spiteful behaviour and they would have to face him if they disrespected me. When Neville heard what Judas P had done he was livid because this was a little boy we had brought up in the business, and we were good friends with his older brother.

The next day I got a rental car and started off-loading the stuff. Next stop would be Judas P's house. He lived down in Kennington on the 21st floor in some high rise block of flats. It was Mr Pang's first visit to England; he did not know London so when I pulled up outside Judas P's house I told him that an old time girlfriend lived there. I knew what would have happen if Pang had gone in because Judas P did not even know that I was in the country, much less that Pang was here on a mission to kill him. Pang would have just done what he came to do and we would have simply flown out of the country. But I also hoped to myself that when Judas P saw me he would just deal with the matter appropriately and saved himself from what would

118

have been a fatal end. I arrived at his front door after what seemed like an eternity in the lift. Mr Pang remained in the car unaware of the fact that it was the snake that he had come to deal with that I had gone to see. I pressed the doorbell twice and after a while he looked through his peep hole and opened the door. He is a brown skinned brother but by now he had turned white and started to stutter. It was like he had seen a ghost.

I stepped past him and went inside, checking out if he was on his own. He managed to compose himself a little and asked, still rather nervously, when I had flown in. I replied, "Forget about that. What happen to the boss bracelet and my money?" He was dumbstruck. Then he started to talk some nonsense and even had the bottle to ask me if I had brought in any high grade because we had promised that this would be a continuous thing. I said, "Yes, it would have been if you did successfully keep to the arrangement we had." By this time I was seeing red, so I told him what I felt like doing to him. Now listen to what this individual said to me; he told me that if I went on threatening and intimidating him he was **going to inform the feds (police) and customs that I was bringing in high grade weed into the country!** I said to him, "You must be on coke! Open your door and let me out before I do you something in here. And by the way, don't come back to Jamaica and let me find out, otherwise you are coming back in a body bag." He stood there in silence and I made my way back to the car. I was now in two minds; do I turn Pang loose on him, or do I leave him to God? I didn't want the blood of this snake on my hands so I jumped back into the car, stunned at what I had just heard.

Mr Pang looked at me as I drove off in silence. "What happen, Chabba, your old time girl dis you?" I did not answer him until I got back to Brixton. I turned and said to him, "Is the boy Judas P I just check." Immediately he turned to me with that menacing look on his face. "So what, you get the money?" I replied, "No." He said, "What you mean, no?" I told him what the degenerate had said. Pang shuffled in his seat and said, "Turn the car 'round, we goin' back – just tell me the number and ah will do the rest." I replied, "Pang, leave that, we have work with us, we can't afford to get busted." He went mad: "NO BWOY DISSING YOU AND THE BOSS LIKE DAT AND LIVE FI TELL THE TALE!"

We spent a total of eight days in London within which time we finished off the work and rescheduled our flights before leaving. Every day of the time we stayed, Pang just wanted to pay Judas P a visit. He didn't know how close he came to being wasted, but I had mercy on him. God had spoken to me and I was going to live to see him get his comeuppance without me even having to lift a finger. I know some of you are wondering what Judas P's true identity is but you will have to keep on wondering unless you can solve this mystery.

My involvement with the dark side of life did not end there. Back in Jamaica, my sound, Destiny, was loved and had a wide range of followers, consisting of the good, the bad, police, soldier, young, old, Socialists (supporters of the PNP – People's National Party), Labourites (supporters of Edward Seaga's Labour Party) as well as members of the now defunct Marxist party, WPJ (Workers Party of Jamaica, which was the then third political party). Now one of the unique things about Destiny was that people from all these walks of life would come to Destiny dances and feel relatively safe, which was not so with many of the other top sounds. The reason was that many of the other sounds were branded as being either Socialist or Labourite sounds, depending on the area they came from. Destiny, however, was neither. We played for anyone and made it crystal clear to all entertainers that Destiny was not a political sound. Despite that, though, it was evident that we had a large number of Socialists following our sound, and this could give any bad minded person the opportunity to spread rumours pertaining to this, which could be detrimental to our safety.

In Mandeville the Socialists and Labourites did not too like each other, just as in most of the island, and I was about to get a taste of their on-going political feud. I played against a sound from the parish of **St Elizabeth** called **Black Organ** and, as was normal, I disposed of him. Little did I know that the owner was a staunch Labour supporter and because of the beating I gave him, he started to stir up rumour among some heavy political bad men that Destiny was a big Socialist sound.

One day as I was walking through Mandeville, a Labourite bad man, called Panton, who always used to listen to my sound, bawls out, "YOO!" Well, as I am not a Chinaman, and if you answer a call like that, man will take you for a joke, I just carried on walking. By this time, seeing that I am not taking the check, he runs up to me, "You ah hear me, Destiny? My boss wants to talk to you." Within a few seconds I see a tall slim menacing looking brother appear and Panton said to him, "Yes, boss, ah this brother own Destiny." He looked at me from head to toe. In a cold voice he said, "You ah hear me? Man fi careful how them whole lot of Socialist following your sound, yu know. It can cause your sound to get shoot up, for you know sey is we, Labourites, ah run things."

Here we go, I was going to have to defend this, or they would have me as a sap, as soft. I turned and said to the boss, "Yu hear me, bredrin, Destiny is not a politics sound; I play for anyone. I don't mix up in your politics so leave me outa dem kind of argument." He raised his arm to let me see the 9mm chrome semi-automatic (gun) he was carrying on him and walked off without saying another word. Panton stood there still and said, "Hey, Destiny, you fi mind how you talk to the boss, them man don't take check." I turned to Panton and said, "I am not going make no man bait up my sound, or be intimidated, cause I am not in no war with nobody." He screwed up his face and walked off. For quite some time the talk was going around, that "Destiny ah socialist sound" and "Better don't go in no Labourite area and play or ah pure war." There were many that loved Destiny and I had a crew of hardcore soldiers that followed the sound. Now these fellows did not play and when they came to my dances and the music I was selecting 'sweet them', they would just empty the magazine of their guns in the air, giving the sound a gun salute.

Somehow, **Mitchey**, who was one of these bad boy soldiers, heard what had gone down. He knew I had a dance coming up in a Labourite area soon so he came and checked me at my base. He said, "Chabba, me hear some Labourite boy them ah run off them mouth, say Destiny cannot play in them area. What are you deciding to do because right now if you want to play them can't stop you ca' me and the crew ah back you to the max." I had to go and play otherwise these men would take set on me (harass me) and take liberties with Destiny.

The night of the dance arrived and my crew are on their guard. I saw some area men come in to check out how heavy we were. They left and returned later, all tooled up. Shortly after that Mitchey (my soldier friend) and some more soldiers pulled up into the dance yard in a well tinted 4x4 jeep, every man of them wearing dark glasses. They came out of the vehicle and the gate man 'dressed back' as they filed in. Mitchey, Shanks, and Dave came up to me at the control and asked me if everything was cool. I replied that it was and they asked me if I wanted something to drink. They bought a crate of Heineken and put it in front of the sound, for which I thanked them, even though I personally don't drink beer. Mitchey then advised me, "You hear me? We are over in that corner, just gwaan mash up the dance." About an hour later I played a Half Pint special and I heard one of the area bad men (Labourite) 'bust a shot' in the air. It sounded like a 38 (a small gun). The next tune I played was a favourite of the soldier crew. *Who told me to do that!* The next thing I heard was when the AKs and the Sixteens[5] opened up. Shots galore were firing from bigger things than

---

[5] AK-47 and M-16 rifles

what the area bad men were carrying. They promptly left the dance, vacating the scene, fast. Mitchey and crew, whenever they attended my dances and I am 'busting selection and the deejay is tearing it down' would usually come and fire the guns right over my head into the air. Sometimes I did not expect it and it would make me jump! (Smile).

Within no time the threatening messages stopped and I continued to play as usual for anyone who wanted to hire the sound, regardless of their political persuasion. I returned to business as normal.

Of the countless number of 'dark' incidents I have experienced, my first brush with a member of the **Jamaican Police Force** could have been fatal for me.

In the area where I lived, me and my step-brother opened a bar and grocery shop, and on any weekend that Destiny was not playing out, we would set up the sound and sell drinks and soup. One Friday night I was packing up the records, shortly before turning off the sound at about 3am in the morning. In those days, I was a big herbalist – smoking 'the most' high grade. That night I had a spliff in my mouth and my back was turned to the dancers who had remained behind still. The next thing I knew, a hand grabbed me with great force in the back of my neck. I remember thinking at the time, 'Ah which idiot doing this?' Immediately, I heard a big crusty voice growling, "HEY BWOY, AH WHA' DIS YU AH SMOKE?!" By now I turned round to see this tall, cranky looking brother who now declared to me that he is a police officer.

I told him that it was a little spliff but he replied, "You don't have no respect, I'm going to lock you up." I then remembered that I had about an ounce of high grade in my pocket, plus my big buck knife. So if this police officer is going on about the spliff in my mouth, what would he say when he got round to searching me and finding more ganja and the knife?

He let me go for a moment but grabbed hold of one of my deejay friends called Joker Irie, and said to him, "Give me a search, bwoy." Time for me to think fast. I took a small step away but I could not afford to let him be aware of what I was doing so while he was checking Joker, I eased the ganja out of my pocket neatly and dropped it to the ground. Within seconds he turned back to me, ready to search me. I said to him, "Before you search me I have my knife in my waist," raising my shirt slowly to show him. But he shouted, "DON'T MOVE BWOY, I WILL SHOT YOU," and he pulled his 45 fast and aimed it at my head. "Take it easy, officer," I said. This policeman seemed trigger happy and definitely ready to squeeze the trigger. You see, some Jamaican police are cool about ganja and others are not. This was one of them. He raised his gun and I heard another voice say, "Malav, don't bother with that. That guy is cool, man."

The other voice was that of his superior officer who I did not know at the time, but he went to school with my step-brother. He also knew that I was the big selector for Destiny sound as he had been to several of our dances and had taken a real liking to the sound. He came closer to me and said, "My name is Detective Jones and you know that you should not be smoking the herb in public suh." He then called Malav to one side and whispered something in his ears. Malav put his gun away and said to me, "You are lucky, boy. I was going to lock you up but Jones says he love your sound so just go hold it down." And the two of them jumped into their car and drove off. What I never dreamt was that this same police officer was going to make my life a misery for a long time.

Several months later, this same officer called Malav came to one of my dances and out of all the girls in the dance, he chose to ask my girl for a dance. This was going to be the start of a nightmare. When he asked her, my girl refused to dance with him and he asked her why. She replied, "Because you was going to lock up my man and pointed your gun on him." Malav now asked her, "Who is your man?" She pointed towards the sound and said, "The selector, Chabba." If you know Jamaican police you will be aware that the bad boy ones don't take lightly to rejection from a girl.

Now in his mind he was going to make my life a misery, and so the drama began. I was on my way from town on a mini bus and ran into a police road block. Guess who was in charge? Yes, Malav. He looked into the mini bus and saw me. He did not even look at another person. "COME OUT," he ordered me. I came out of the mini bus and he grabbed me and said, "Have you got any GANJA on you?" I said no, and he started to search me. "Let me find *one seed* on you and I will show you something, today." He found a large amount of cash. "Where did you get so much money from?" I felt like saying, your girl, but I know that would have been silly so I calmly asked him, "Are you forgetting that I am a business man?" Hear the thief, "So what, let off something 'pon me." Because I knew how these hungry belly police flexed, I give him a change and he quickly put it in his pocket and warned me, "You can gwaan but I am watching you." Straightaway I said to myself that this was going to be a problem, all because he did not get to lock me up, then my girl refused to dance with him. This was going to be a constant cat and mouse thing. He harassed me again on several other occasions, even intimidating me with his legal gun.

During the time of Destiny there were quite a few bad boy police officers that would follow the sound and this was how I was going to eventually get rid of Malav. After several more incidents it got to a stage that if I saw him first I would divert, just to avoid him. A notorious police officer was running Mandeville hot, and again, through the sound me and him became good friends. His name was **Sammy Dread** and he loved Destiny sound with a passion. One day he and I were talking when Malav's name came up. I started to tell Sammy how he was behaving. He looked at me and asked why I did not tell him before how the boy was behaving and he got quite upset. His final words were, "Watch me and him when I see him!" Another officer who I knew later gave me the drama about how Sammy dealt with Malav. He said Sammy told him, "You ah hear me? You see anywhere you see Chabba, don't even look pon him otherwise me ah go deal with you. Remember, Malav, say I don't play. Chabba ah good youth so leave him alone." He said Malav just stood there like a baby and apologized. From that day Malav would see me and pretend that he didn't. I had used one of his own to get rid of him.

There was another murderer police I knew also, called **Bagga**. He came from my area, originally, and he also warned Malav on another occasion. These officers I am telling you about took it as being part of their job to wipe out a man as if it was nothing, for they could not take the softly-softly approach otherwise rude boys would wipe them out. The last officer I am going to speak about was not a friend of mine but an out and out killer named **Ashman**. One day Ashman arrested two local bad boys in connection with some robbery. He questioned the first one and after a short while he shot him four times in his head. This he did in full view of the other friend and everyone who was on the scene. He started to seek information from the other friend, making him feel that if he talked he was going to spare him. The other youth started to give him some information but Ashman just stopped him and said, "I had this for you anyway," and just emptied the rest of the bullets into the youth with not even blink. Cold hearted.

You see, there were both good and bad experiences of my time living in Jamaica. It was like being at school. I tell you one thing, if you can live in Jamaica, where the fittest of the fittest survives, you can live anywhere. Likewise, my experience of functioning Destiny sound system in Jamaica has increased not only my confidence in that business but also my knowledge of competition, and most importantly, people.

After taking the scalp of GT International, my in-house entertainers were getting hotter by the day and lots of sounds were on their guard against us. Of the defeated sounds I have mentioned so far, the great **Stone Love** has not been among them because in those days they were just a little party sound and did not have the worldwide recognition as they do now.

The great legendary selector, **Sky Juice** was another of my victims. In those days he was selecting for a sound called **Black Zodiac** before he started playing with **Metro Media**. My bonafide, Sugar Minott, kept a dance in Kingston at Chisholm Avenue with Destiny and Black Zodiac. I destroyed Sky Juice so that he had to lock off his sound and all his entertainers came over to Destiny. I can remember one of the main tunes I used to vanquish him – it was a Barry Brown tune called **Thank You Mama**. This was before the GT dance; I am talking a year earlier, in 1984. Destiny has done its fair share of killing sounds, so much so that some even slip my mind.

My next focus was to increase the size of Destiny and to start recording my artistes before they got despondent and moved on, because everyone in the music business wanted to become famous; no one wanted to be what we would call, an iron balloon. The problem I was having was that Copper, my step-brother, was not as fully focused as I was and did not know the business like me. He was too busy playing around with these young girls who were running him down because he owned a big sound shop, along with a bar, and had a lovely house. In fact, quite a few mature women were also hot on his heels.

When you are a celebrity it is very easy to get carried away and lose focus. This could have happen to me, too, because if they were chasing him can you imagine me the big time selector and part owner of Destiny? There were times I would have to hide after the dance because there was a line of girls waiting to go home with me. These young ladies did not take prisoners – they demanded the wickedest slam!

At this point in my life I still had not fathered my first child yet, but all of that was soon to change. It was the tale end of 1985 and my girlfriend became pregnant. This caused bitter resentment from many other girls who wanted to be in this position. There were those who threatened to do all manner of evil because a prize catch had gotten away as far as they were concerned. I could have been like many other celebrities who had children all over the place with many different women, but thank the good Lord I did not.

At this time, as you can imagine, Destiny's popularity was soaring beyond belief. The entertainers like Kulcha Knox, Bimbo (Garnett Silk), Tony Rebel, and Everton Blender were in demand. All I had in my intention, sound-wise, was to take Destiny to a higher level. Likewise, each person has their own quest and in life there are times when we reach a crossroad which often means searching for our true identity and direction.

I could see that something was troubling Bimbo and I asked him about it. As I said earlier, Bimbo saw me as his bigger brother and his mentor. He confided in me and told me that he had met some Mormons in Mandeville and they told him about their religion and had invited him to their church. He said he liked how they spoke and if you knew Garnett Silk on a personal level, you would know he always had a godly presence about him and wanted to draw nearer to the Lord. I advised him that it was something one had to feel comfortable with in their own spirit and no man could make that decision for him. After a few days of thinking about it he came back to me. He told me that he was not going to take this Mormon theology any further and that was the last he spoke of it, and religion, until he eventually followed the Rastafari doctrine after he became known as **Garnett Silk.** There are very few who knew Garnett Silk on the close and personal level that I did. His mother and I also got on very well. She was grateful that her son had found a positive friend and role model like me in his life. To this very day I find it hard to come to terms with the fact that he is no longer here with us in the physical sense. By then I had moved back to England and Destiny sound was no more, but his death (in 1994) hit me hard at the time.

In the year 1986 we were planning to take the sound off the road for a period of time to do some refurbishment and increase its size. I played a few more dances, even having a big clash with **Papa San's** sound that he was resident on at the time, a sound called **Creation Rock Tower.** This sound was from **Spanish Town** and was owned by a woman – yes, a woman, named **Mama G** whose daughter (I don't remember her name) was one of Papa San's girls. Papa San also worked on Destiny sound at one of our dances over at Westmorland. He used to be a firm favourite with the Westmorland people.

This clash with Creation was brutal. By now I was also friends with the great **No Wanga Gut, No Wanga Belly**, yes, the great **Tiger,** and he was working alongside my crew that night. No doubt Papa San was a crucial deejay but my crew and Tiger was too much for him and his brother, Dirtsman. The woman that owned Creation was very full of herself, so I dealt with her sound accordingly – giving them a right good beating and sending them back to Spanish Town.

The big don and I were still close, even though Judas P did what he did, so certain things were still running. We played the last dance before we pulled the sound off the road. Now my step-brother with whom I owned Destiny was now a partner in another business as I had now enlightened him about the smuggling and wanted him to have a lucrative cut of things. The plan was that he would carry a certain amount up to London and stay there for six months working it in small quantities in order to gain maximum profit. We would send two consignments while he was there and he was suppose to send my and the boss' share of the money to Jamaica. This was to be a familiar story in my life about to repeat itself. I was going to be stung again and could end up dead.

I should say that it was never my intention to start smuggling, but one of my dreams was to build my own house in Jamaica so the funds that I would accumulate from this would go towards that project. I was also aware that this would not last forever and that the money from this venture was not clean and could be gone in the twinkling of an eye.

My step-brother left for England fully loaded and I was left holding the fort. I played a couple more dances as a few more dates came in. Our entertainers could not believe how well they were paid, and with no hassle, all because I was paying them now and not Copper, who liked to short change people. I often would argue with him about this nasty habit of his but he would laugh and say that I am too kind. After a few months of him leaving there was little contact from him and no money was being sent over, even though I had sent through two consignments of high grade which went through without a hitch.

By now, again, my boss, to whom part of the work belonged, said, "Chabba, what is Copper dealing with? It looks like this is a next Judas P thing!" I was embarrassed again. Furthermore, if this did turn out to be another "Judas P thing", would the boss see it that I just involved the wrong person again, or would he see it as a conspiracy? For the second time my life was on the line. The boss said, "Hear what, take a trip over and check out things." I would also be carrying a consignment with me.

In May of 1986 I flew into Heathrow airport. This was the second time that I was going to beat the customs and come through. I reached

130

Brixton and checked Neville, my trustworthy friend, and again he filled me in on what had been going on. He told me that my step-brother was going on as if he was the big don, making a killing with the high grade and talking some terrible lies about me.

The only person who knew I was in town was Neville. It was now time to pay Copper a surprise visit for as far as he was concerned, I was down in Jamaica. I quickly hired a rental car and drove down to check my step-brother who was staying at my Dad's house. Just like Judas P, he was so shocked when he saw me, but without any long argument I said, "What's all this that you been talking about me?" Well, you can imagine, he denied everything and wanted to know if I had work with me. I didn't even answer him. Instead, I demanded to know where the money was that he was supposed to send down to Jamaica for me and the boss. He claimed that because of the large amount of cash he did not want to keep it with him so he sent it down to the bank in Jamaica. I told him to make sure to give the boss his money as soon as possible and he told me that he would give me mine on his return.

I quickly began to realize how devious Copper was for this deviousness would result in the end of our business venture and nearly resulted in his death. I spent a couple of weeks and got rid of my consignment which I had brought over. After this the first thing I did was to buy everything that my soon coming child would need, except for a cot. When I left London I did not even tell him.

By this time it was June 1986 and with it came one of the most terrible **tropical storms** to hit Jamaica, resulting in lots of flooding. My in-laws were saying all kind of things because my girl was about to give birth and they did not see any movement by me to make provision. They had forgotten that Chabba moved under cover so when it became apparent on my return, and they saw how well she and my expectant child were provided for, they had to eat their words.

After a month of my return, my step-brother returned from England and I and one of my crew picked him up from the airport. For the entire journey back we did not exchange three words between us. Everything was tense until we reached Mandeville. I decided then to watch him to see what he was dealing with.

On the **14th August, 1986**, my girl gave birth to a beautiful baby girl at Mandeville hospital; my daughter and first born child, **Anecia.** However, I found out about it that morning when I arrived home after playing out at a dance, so it was a pleasant surprise for me.

I was now a dad and many girls were upset because it meant I would not be available to them. Copper still had not said anything that made sense to me. We lived in the same house but were literally passing each other like strangers. I told myself that this was enough and so I confronted him. I said, "Copper we need to talk." Incredibly, he turned to me and said, "What about?" Can you believe this man? He owed me thousands of pounds, plus we had the sound to sort out and he answered me like that! I got mad: "What do you mean, 'what about'? I retorted. "Firstly, what's happening with my money, plus secondly, what are we doing with the sound?" He then pulled off what he thought was his stunt, accusing me of being a thief. I asked him, "I have been out here with you all these years and it is just now you know that I am a thief" By now I have lost it and said to him, "You ah hear me? I am leaving out here because I can see it will be either I kill you or you kill me. And by the way, I have to get my things because you must be on coke or you gone insane."

As I walked out of the house all kinds of evil thoughts were running through my head. One mind was saying "go and get my bredrin gun and shoot him". Then God spoke to me and reminded me that he is my step-mum's son and she was a person who never treated me like I was not her child. God reminded me that my Mother could not take any more bad news as my other brother was now missing over a year with no trace of him. Finally, God reminded me of the most important thing – to leave vengeance to Him and to forgive. When I thought about it all, I said to myself, 'Well, maybe I will leave the vengeance to you, God. But the forgiving part? Well, that I did not learn how to do – until I become a Born Again Christian, many years later. For this, thank you JESUS.

When I left the house, I made my way to a close friend and when he saw the look on my face he asked, "What happen, who trouble you, Chabba?" Tears of anger were running down my cheeks. I still had not answered my friend and when I finally told him he went ballistic: "Ah whe di bwoy, Copper deh?!" he asked. "Me ah go deal with him, ah big disrespect that!" My friend was not referring to talking to him; he was going to burn his skin (shoot him). I knew my friend was feeling the anger and disappointment which I was feeling and at that point all I wanted was some kind of revenge because this was a cold-hearted move by my step-brother.

By the next day several more of my close friends had gotten wind of what had gone down and they came to link me up. Every one of them was mad. What made it worse was that they did not feel Copper's vibes from day one. They said, "Chabba, just say the word and we will fly his head and go and dump him." The voice of the devil was saying in my head, 'Yea, let them brush him,' while the Voice of God said, 'No, do not let them kill him. Forgive him for he knows not what he has done.'

Day and night for weeks I was tormented with my thoughts. All my hard work had been wasted and my dreams had been shattered, all because of this man's greed. But most of all, I now had a child to feed. One thing I was determined on was that even if I didn't get the money which was due to me, my equipment, which was half of the total sound, was in no way going to him; he would have to kill me first.

After I walked out, I realised that there were some sound dates that were already booked and could not be cancelled, for deposits had already been taken. My step-brother was now in a serious dilemma because he could not tell the multitude of people the truth as to why I left and why he was not playing the sound anymore. Furthermore, just like when I left Soferno-B, the main heartbeat had gone and Destiny was bound to flop. He, however, thought that Destiny was able to continue making headway without me, but how wrong and fatal this was going to turn out to be in more ways than one.

Copper's attempts to play the first dance without me to select for the sound was a shambles. A friend told me that there was no vibes and the sound was not up to its usual quality. The entertainers working that night had no vibes and the replacement selector was totally inadequate. The dancers were on their case, shouting, "Where is **Chabba Melo**?" Copper hid in a corner in the dance all night, regularly chain smoked, and had "a face expression like you know what." This was not looking good for him and Destiny. He had just wrecked one of the greatest sounds which would have come out of Jamaica and had also just lost a gold mine, all because of his greed.

He attempted to play a few more dances but by now it was time for me to withdraw my share of the equipment. However, even though he had done this terrible thing to me, I still agreed to let him honour the existing dates which were booked. The agreement was that after these dates, I would be paid a percentage and then collect my equipment. By now the entertainers like Kulcha Knox, Garnett Silk, Tony Rebel, and Everton Blender were completely disgusted at what Copper had done to me and they all decide that they would move on in order to further their careers. Tony Rebel became a regular on the sound of my long time friend, Sugar Minott, which was called **Youth Promotion** and he encouraged Garnett Silk to accompany him in dances, mostly in Kingston. Kulcha Knox and Everton Blender were now going over to some big name producers in the business and their rapid rise to fame is now history.

Chapter 8

THICK AND THIN

As time went on, more and more people were hearing of the break-up and I could not go anywhere in peace without someone coming up to me wanting to know what had happened with Destiny and the falling out between me and Copper.

Remember the police officer I told you about, Sammy Dread who loved Destiny with a passion? He found out that Destiny was no more to be and he was fuming for several weeks, I had to avoid him. When Jamaicans love you, a fly cannot pitch on you and they support you to the max, but when they hate you, you might as well be dead. Anyway, the day came when Sammy Dread finally caught up with me and I explained to him. All I can say is that Copper was one lucky individual for Sammy was gutted; he was very fond of me. He said, "Let me pay him a visit," but I knew it would not have been, let me say, 'nice'. All I had to do was to say the word. From the first day of my arrival in Jamaica the massive took a real liking to me because of the type of person I was and because I knew how to live amongst people.

The day was hot as I made my way to collect my equipment from Copper at the time we had agreed. When I got to the house he switched on me again with the most ridiculous talk, saying that I cannot get anything because he is taking all my equipment and I can do what I feel to do. 'Here we go again,' I thought. 'This man is playing with fire – he really has a death wish.' This idiot was not satisfied with stealing my money; he wanted everything that I owned.

I said to him, "Now I know that you are out of your head. Watch this ride, I will be back."

I headed straight to Mandeville police station and checked one of my hardcore police friends. At this point I had to be seen as doing things according to the law so that when the mess hits the fan all things have been documented. After explaining to my police friend what had happened he said, "Copper must be drinking mad puss piss (gone mentally insane); come, we are going up there." When we got to the house my friend knocked on the door and Copper's sister, who was now staying there, answered the door. The police officer asked where he was and she replied that he had gone out, which was a lie for he was hiding round the back. My police friend said to her, "Hear me and hear me good. Tell Copper let Chabba get his things without any further delay, and tell him that I said don't let me have to come back here again, otherwise he knows how it is going to go." Then we left. On the way driving back to the station we had a good laugh because we knew that the little rat was hiding and he knew that my friend did not 'skin teeth', he was very serious. The officer then advised me, "Meet me at the station in the morning, early, we going to pay him a surprise visit."

The next morning, bright and early, as I stood by the station gate, who do I see coming out of a taxi and beckoning me to come to him? I walked over to him and he said, "I don't want any trouble, I will be back home in a hour you can come and get your equipment." I said to him, "Make sure because you know I am not playing any more games." He looked at me with fear in his eyes and got back into the taxi.

An hour passed and I and another friend went with a truck to pick up my equipment. Copper was standing at the front of the house and he kept on watching to see if my police friend was going to show up. He had even stolen my specials, my exclusive records, which I had cut with my own money for Destiny. The main thing was that I got my equipment for he was not having them – full stop.

That episode was now water under the bridge. I was now back to square one – no money, flat broke, with a woman and child to feed and rent to pay.

One of my other close friends was running a body workshop, repairing crashed cars, and he said to me, "Chabba you have to eat an' even though you don't know how to do body work, come an' help me so you can hustle a change." The one time big selector was now going to have to eat humble pie, forget about his pride and do what he had to do to survive – this was yard!

Chabba and Peckman Stirling

Within a short space of time I was learning how to prepare a car for spraying, how to do welding, and getting a little change at the same time. Meanwhile, that boy, Copper, was flossing it with my money that he had robbed from me. And so the devil turned up the heat with

138

the mind games he pushes onto one, such as: 'You can't let this happen to you; what is people going to think? The great Chabba Melo has gone soft? Go and sort him out,' or, 'Why don't you set up a big drugs move and get back in the grove? You did it before you can do it again.' Had it not been for my strong will power, I would have gotten involved again but I had to stay focused for the sake of my woman and child. A guiding voice said: 'DON'T DO IT, CHABBA. TRUST IN ME.'

After a period of time I knew I would have to make a move back to England because this is my original turf and I could manipulate what needed to be done to set a future for myself and my new Family. So the next thing was to raise some money to book a flight. There were people that I could have gone to but my pride and not wanting to have to bother anyone prevented me. One of the many experiences from which I have learnt in life is that some people will help you and then 'chat' you behind your back, or they will have an ulterior motive for helping you. But the question was still there, where was I going to get this money from? This was a nightmare, but one thing I believed was that God would work something out for me. He had seen my needs and, as I said, at that time I did not know that the Lord was preparing me for the calling that He had for me later.

Then one day a thought came to me that a certain person who should have done things to help in the past, but did not do so, should now be my help. So I wrote a letter to him explaining the situation and telling him that I knew that he was in a position to help me and if he did not then he could cut all ties with me. I made it known that it was just a loan I wanted until I got back on my feet. This might sound harsh to you, dear reader, but this person owed me big time. I will not say who it was as some things are best not said, but one thing you can be certain of, it was not Judas P. This person in question did a search of his conscience and replied to my letter, saying that I was just to let him know when I wanted to travel. Thank you, Jesus!

My next hurdle, now that I had a ticket in place, was how to find some money to leave for my woman and baby daughter to keep them financially until I could go to set things in motion. My mind was doing overtime but I was thankful that God had made me able to handle extreme pressure and I needed to display this ability now more than ever before. My alternative plan, if I could not raise sufficient money to leave for them, was to leave with my woman and child. I would just have to trust and believe in God that within a short time of returning to England, I would get a job to enable me to maintain them while I work and save in the fastest time possible and return to bring them back to England with me.

One of the last pieces of the jigsaw puzzle would be every man's concern – could I trust this woman? This thought was pressing on me, especially as I don't know the length of time I would be away and a lot of men would love to boast that they have been with Chabba's woman. Well, it would have to be up to her. Any game could play, but I felt confident so I put my trust in her. All I knew was that I had to move in order to get back on my feet. She and I had many heartfelt discussions and there were, as you can imagine, some tearful moments. The question that kept running through both of our minds was, would we ever see each other again, and would I have a presence in my daughter's life. This was some serious food for thought.

Just before I left to return to England, there was a sound called **Red Rose** which hailed from **Porus**, an area in Manchester, not far from Mandeville. The owner of Red Rose sound was a big don called Jah Vin, who would spend most of his time travelling between New York and Jamaica. Anytime he was out of the island his sound would be off the road for he struggled to find a good selector, and for the sound to gather momentum.

Jah Vin had always admired Destiny sound and loved how I selected for it, so when he heard that I was no longer selecting for Destiny he approached me to select for Red Rose.

After a few initial meetings with him I decided to select for Red Rose sound. Within a very short space of time, Red Rose sound had undergone a complete transformation and now Jah Vin was getting the recognition he had always craved. This was the first time since he started his sound that he began to make some financial gain from it, of which he made no secret. I selected for his sound for several dances all over the island, one of which was kept at the famous **Jack Ruby** lawn. However, this was only going to be a short-lived affair as we had a difference of opinion on one of my major business principles. I could not play a sound who worked on a shoestring budget when it came to buying music for the sound. This was also a major problem I faced with Copper buying for Destiny. I, on the other hand, would spend my last pound on music for my sound, and often did, to our ultimate benefit; but there are those who are not willing to go to that extent. This was so with Red Rose so I left. Shortly afterwards, Jah Vin pleaded with me to return but his willingness to be constantly cutting music in the studios was not the same as mine, plus he needed to increase my personal salary as good selectors do not come cheap.

We were now in 1987. The time was fast approaching when I would leave Jamaica to return to England to start all over again. This was not a good time for me emotionally; things were in ruins despite all the hard work I had put in. One of my ambitions was to build a house for myself in Jamaica. I had started to do so but after completing the first stages, I had to abandon it, thereby losing a large sum of cash – all because of the self-greed of Copper. Then there were the many close friends I had made over the years. It was hard to come to terms with leaving them. And of course, my sound colleagues, artists like Kulcha Knox, Garnett Silk, Everton Blender, Tony Rebel, and several more I was going to miss. It was a pity that what we should have achieved together had now come to an end.

The night before I was due to fly out was one of the most heartbreaking times of my life. I sat with my baby daughter in my arms, just looking at her and wondering what was going to be the outcome. I held my woman tight, trying my best to assure her that if she had faith in God and trusted me, everything would eventually be alright. Nevertheless, this was some pill to swallow. The money that I had to leave with them was very minimal. I remember thinking to myself that I am going to need a miracle to make things work, but all the time I was trusting in God. Nevertheless, that night seemed like one of the longest nights I had ever known.

It was now morning and the moment I dreaded most, saying goodbye, had arrived. I wanted to cry but I had to put on a brave face and stay focused. My driver sounded his horn outside the house and I put my case in the back of the car before taking one long, hard look at my surroundings. There was a lump in my throat and I swallowed hard. I could see the sadness by the expression on my woman's face, and even my little daughter, at that tender age; it was as if she knew that her daddy was going away. The three of us got into the car and I had to dig deep to control my emotions. On the way to the airport, my memories were flooding back thick and fast. There was not much talking on the way just an influx of mixed emotions and one thing I was certain of was that the breath would have to leave my body before I would give up.

After this somewhat emotional drive to Kingston we reached Norman Manley Airport. My heart was pounding faster than ever. I was thinking, 'This is for real and in a short while I will be boarding this flight, leaving behind two of the most important people in my life. Life is a real bitch!' When it was time to enter Departures, I gave my woman a final hug and kiss before whispering gently in her ear, "Just pray for me and ask the good Lord to protect me." Even though at this time I never dreamt that I would become a Born Again Christian, let alone be ordained as a minister for Christ, I always would have my Bible with me for I knew there is a Creator.

After waving goodbye I entered Departures. It was a good thing on this occasion that I was not carrying anything else; I got to realize now how fortunate I was previously before because of the intensity of the search they gave me now – I had never encountered the like before. Maybe it was because they could still smell the odour of the high grade on my clothes because that morning I made sure of one last big-head spliff. In those days I was a top herb smoker and very few could keep up with me.

For example, one day I went up to Westmoreland and visited a friend who was a ganja farmer. Anyone who knows about Jamaican ganja can confirm that Westmoreland is where one of the most potent high grade is grown. I had exchanged some goods with him and he gave me two and a half pound weight of ses (high grade ganja) which I travelled back to Mandeville with. This herb was so potent that it produced a smell that was too high to travel inside the bus with me. I had to take a country bus with a roof rack and put it on the roof rack to travel. Apart from one ounce of this high grade which I gave a to a friend to sell, both Copper and I completely smoked off the rest. We use to see who could smoke the most and he could not keep up with me. The other smokers in the area use to ask how I could burn the ganja in the middle of the day and did not get smashed, especially with the sun's heat beating down. "Man ah herbalist", they would say. So you see, smoking weed was my thing and I could handle it but my women used to beg me to slow down. I have become wiser now, though, and know that everything is but for a time. One should know when enough is enough and it was not the right thing for me to be doing so all you apprentices out there, quit now before it quits you.

Chapter 9

RETURN TO ENGLAND

After the body search, I waited in the departure lounge. It all just seemed like a dream and I would soon wake up. But it was not, I really was heading back to England, to an uncertain future. There were those who were going to be glad to see me, most of all my Mother, and there were the others, such as the haters, who would be casting all kinds of aspersions as to why I was back in town. At one stage there were rumours going around in England that I had become mentally ill and was walking around feeding from garbage bins in Jamaica. That is how cruel and evil mankind can be, especially when they don't know your business. My main concern was my woman and child which I had left behind, not knowing how quickly I would be able to get things up and running.

On my arrival in London, my first stop, as usual, was my Mother's house where my old room was still vacant. What a reunion! If someone had given her a million pounds she could not have been more pleased. This was a very emotional time for both me and my Mother because our reunion highlighted the fact that my eldest brother, as I mentioned earlier on, had disappeared without a trace for the past four years. The speculations about his absence were very disturbing to say the least and to this very day we are none the wiser as to where he is. I used to hear people speak of missing loved ones but I can relate to how they feel. My brother's name is Delroy. He was a popular person, known to many at the time as a loveable rogue. The last time I saw him was May 1985 when I returned from Jamaica for a couple of months before going back to continue my quest. This has been another difficult ongoing chapter in my life; still an emotional rollercoaster. Nevertheless, God is good.

After my reunion with Mum my next stop was to catch up with my life long bredrin, Neville, co-owner of Stereograph. He would fill me in on what was going on. My mind had no time to rest as I needed to start earning some money fast. I had a child and a woman to support so I had to get my act together quickly. Monday morning arrived and I went down to the Job Centre to see what was on offer. There was nothing of any great significance so I bought the South London Press to check out the local 'Jobs' page. One particular advert caught my eye: "Security guards wanted to do CIT duties" at a company called Pritchards on Wandsworth Road. CIT stands for cash-in-transit and refers to the job performed by security guards who go into banks and business places to collect and transport cash.

I called the number and arranged to attend an interview the very next day, which was the Tuesday. Bearing in mind that I had just arrived the Sunday I was not doing too badly, being able to land my first job interview two days later. The only thing on my mind was that I needed to get this job. After speaking with the manager he seemed to warm to me. I was almost there. The wages on offer was £2.50 (two pounds and fifty pence) per hour. I remember thinking that for me to earn a fairly substantial amount of money from this job I would have to work round the clock, and this was virtually what I did. After the manager offered me the job I told him that due to my circumstances I needed to earn a higher wage. He thought for a moment and said that he was willing to offer me double shifts to increase my wage. This is what I had to do in order to clear a hundred pounds a week, after tax.
The next duty I had to do in the evenings, sometimes right throughout the night, was what they called static shift where you would guard a building and patrol on 12 hour shifts. Within the next couple of days I started working and was doing round-the-clock Sunday to Sunday. It got so bad that the only way me and my Mother communicated was

by notes that I would leave on the dining table because she was still working at that time. One day I was using the toilet and fell asleep on it, my Mother had to wake me – that's how exhausted I was.

My target was to accumulate enough money to be able to go and get my woman and child from Jamaica within one year, or just over, and this money had to be clean and legit. However, the devil started to play his usual games, trying to get me involved in certain things. But I stayed focused. The sound business had completely changed in England and those who I had left to deal with Stereograph, my beloved crew, found it hard to maintain the standard in my absence. This was no surprise because my love for sound system went beyond the ordinary and I was the heartbeat and main driving force of Stereograph. You would have to search hard to find those who loved sound system the way I did. Still, all said and done, maximum respect goes out to man like Central, Fizty, Big D, Spinner, Ossie, Dego Ranks, Silver Fox, Marshall Lee, Lascell, Younger Youth (deceased), Slang, Marie Poser, Des, Carl, David, and Terry.

I have learnt that there are those who have real love for something and there are others who love something from a hype point of view or with an ulterior motive – thus two different types of love. The love I had for sound system back in those days was second to none. I would rather be hungry and naked than to know that my sound was in need of something and did not purchase it. I would spend my last on music because my sound or any sound that I selected for had to be in tip-top condition. There were those amongst Soferno-B, Stereograph, and Destiny who said that I spent too much money on music, but you know the sad thing? I asked none of these people for a penny towards anything that I did. This was why many of my rivals in the sound business, both in the UK and Jamaica, were glad to see the back of me. They should be thankful that I have now given my life to the Lord because, trust me, I would still be out there terrorising them.

Anyway, I continued working day and night, and within eleven months I was able to return to Jamaica and bring my woman and daughter back to England to live with me. Many where shocked how quickly this materialised but when God's favour is in your life nothing is impossible. Within a short space of time both of them adjusted to their new life in England and I had moved from strength to strength in my working life. I left the security work and was now working with Kingston-upon-Thames Council as a parking officer with a better salary and working conditions.

In December 1988 the next milestone in my life was to be the birth of my first son, **Jason**. I was a dad again and I gave God thanks and asked for his guidance in this crucial role.

I still had the music in my blood and was getting approached left, right and centre to re-enter the business. However, I just kept on doing my ordinary job, only making the very odd appearance in a dance as I still had a lot of my music selection. Over the years I had lost an unaccountable amount of music, including many irreplaceable tunes, stolen or borrowed and never returned. It sent shivers down my spine when I use to think about it. Some of those collections are worth hundreds of pounds in today's collectors market, as I touch upon further on in this book.

I went back down to Jamaica for a brief visit in 1997 and they were still mourning the death of my champion sound, Destiny, which had taken Jamaica like a storm in 1983 until 1990. Destiny was responsible for bringing to the forefront of reggae music a great number of icons in the business, such as, Garnett Silk, Kulcha Knox, Tony Rebel, Everton Blender, and Shabba Ranks. There are those who do not like to admit it but the truth is the truth; even certain artists when doing interviews never mention the part Destiny and I played in their careers. But that's cool, because there are those who know, and greater still, God knows everything.

My life had changed now from those days in the sound and music world. I was now a family man with different priorities. Nevertheless, every so often the music would return to haunt me, wanting to get me involved again.

However, for a particular time, my mind and heart were taken up with the celebration of the birth of our second son, **Shamar**, now called **Chabba**, in July 1992. He is the spitting image of me (not to say Jason, my first son is not, because from you see all of my children you know, without a shadow of a doubt, that they are my children).

A little while, later on, just after Chabba's birth, someone came back into my life – my long time great friend, none other than the great Sugar Minott. And you can guess what that meant; yes, more involvement in the music/sound business again. Sugar had lost track of me since I returned to England, despite making several attempts to find me, so you can imagine the joy now that he had. The first question he asked me was, "Chabba, are you still selecting sound system, and do you have any equipment?" Before I could reply he went on, "Here is what I would like you to do for me if you can." I listened, hoping it would not be something too demanding and he continued: "I started up a branch of my sound, **Youth Promotion,** and the guys I allow to deal with it are not who I thought them was. Them bringing disgrace to my name because the main guy and some others with him are crack addicts and they are associated with my sound."

Anyone who knew Sugar on a close personal level, like me, would know he did not mix with such things. He continued, "This is what I want you to do. Come and take the entire music selection belonging to the sound and start playing as Youth Promotion for me, because I know that I can trust you and it would not take you long to establish the sound with your status and ability in the business."

I took a deep breath, thinking to myself, 'Do I really want to go back down this road again?' But because of my love and respect for Sugar I decided to see what I could do. This was also to be the start of a solid relationship with his younger brother, **Earl Minott**, who is like one of my brothers to this very day. Well, it did not take long before word got around and a few dates came in. This made Sugar pleased and he returned to continue his work in Jamaica. It was only to be a short space of time before the haters were surfacing again with their knives fully sharpened. The problem they had was that, here I was again in the position of having all this exclusive music at my disposal, which many craved for. I continued with Promotion for a period of time before hanging up my gloves again. I enjoyed it for the while, but my life had now changed with different priorities to deal with.

In 1994, some shattering news reached me concerning the death of one of the greatest artists I had discovered, my protégé, Garnett Silk, aka Bimbo. This hit me severely and for days I could not eat. As I explained earlier, it was me who initially saw his singing potential over his deejaying ability and mentored and coached him through his early singing stage. Again many have taken credit for finding Garnett Silk but there are a few who know the truth, and greater still, God knows.

So where has the music got to since the days of Garnet Silk and his colleagues? There was and still is to some degree the demand for some of the old veteran selectors and sound systems to play at revival dances, playing their old selections and seeing who still has the most exclusive tunes. The great Supertone, aka Wally, decided to keep one of these revival dances at St Matthews church hall in Brixton, inviting the following sounds to play: Sir Coxsone, Fatman, D-Unes, Exodus, I Spy, Frontline, Hawkeye, and, now listen to this, also SOFERNO-B and STEREOGRAPH! What was he thinking? Remember, I was Soferno-B **and** Stereograph. Anyway, I was going to be there as

Stereograph. A couple of jokers turned up to play as Soferno-B, but less said about that.

When I got there several of the other selectors were already in attendance but no man wanted to go first. I did not turn up to play cat and mouse so I said, "Call me in whichever order, it does not matter to me because whatever position I play, damage will be done." Listen to this, after they said I must play after Fatman, Festus (from the Sir Coxsone crew) then decided he wanted to play after me, craving for a chance to get one over on me for past beatings I'd given him years ago. Well, what a big mistake he made. When Stereograph started to play I was the first sound that night to really get the dance fans moving – pure lighters in the air, flashing their approval. I had signed on with one of my classic dub plates from back in the days, a Wailing Souls tune called War, produced by Channel One studio. And the dance erupted. Then came Festus next, with the biggest introductory talk, and then he played this ridiculous instrumental tune which made him look foolish. I can remember it like it was yesterday. Lloyd Coxsone himself was so embarrassed he did not know where to look. Let me set the record straight: Festus was my idol before I started to select. He was one of the all time greats, but he just did not know when to hang up his gloves like a lot of them who are still out there craving for the limelight but punched-drunk like many boxers. This cannot happen to me for I left the business with my reputation intact and my head held high for my past achievements. Even though the haters will not admit it, I ended my career as a champion who vanquished an untold amount of opponents – selectors/sound systems from England to Jamaica (all over) so why ruin this impeccable record?

My small studio, 1994 (Chabba)

Chapter 10

THE OTHER EXTREME OF MY LIFE

The period of my life that I am about to share with you now consists of both the unhappiest and the happiest times of my life. This time began in 1995 when I was totally out of the music scene. My Family life was totally dominant, with three beautiful children and the woman I loved. At this period of time, after having done several jobs I started working with the Royal Mail as a driver, working all hours to try and purchase my own house and secure a future for my Family. It was the same old story; working every hour God sent to make my plans come to past. After several years the good Lord made it possible for me to purchase a house and get my children off the same estate where I had lived for many years before I went to Jamaica to live – the famous Angell Town Estate.

Our new house, which was in Thornton Heath, needed a lot of remedial work – far more than I was initially aware of, but it was away from the area because even if I had wanted it, the prices of properties in Brixton were way out of my budget. We got the house in November 1998 but were not able to move in until April 1999, owing to the amount of work that was needed on it. Every day I had to give God thanks for because of Him we eventually moved in. I can remember the first night that we slept there; my late Father got the Pastor of his church to come and bless our new home and asked for God's protection over us. And guess which church this was; yes, **Shepherd's** Railton Road Methodist Church! After a great number of years, this church was still playing a significant part in my life.

The first few years of this my new life went well. And then all hell broke loose! Firstly, I had an accident whilst at work, thereby sustaining a massive injury to my left ankle which left it severely damaged. The next crisis I was going to face nearly destroyed me both mentally and physically. This began with the break-up of my relationship with my children's mother after nearly 18 years, and then the loss of the home which I'd work so hard to provide. When the relationship ended I left the home and went back to my Mother's house until I could get a place for myself. For the first few months after the split, all three children stayed with their mother. However, later on, Shamar, the youngest, who had always clung to me, came to live with me at my Mother's. After a period of about a year I got a place for myself and I moved out of my Mother's house with Shamar. However, owing to some legal wrangles I lost that as well and had to return once again to my Mother's house.

I was going through mental torment, for the devil was having a field day with my life. But in all of this, God was preparing me for the calling He had determined for me. Anyway, to add more pain to my suffering, one of my older brothers was going through the same thing – family break-up after twenty-odd years of being together with his children's mother. To say we were both bitter would have been an understatement.

I recall in the early stage of our break-ups, and I can laugh about it now, we were both consoling one another in my kitchen and my trousers just fell off my waist, even though I had my belt done up. The amount of weight I had lost was phenomenal, but this is how unhappiness and distress can hit you at times. At this time I was not a nice person to be around. I was very unsociable but the good Lord was watching over me even though I did not know this. A close and dear friend of mine called **Ken** was a rock to me, along with certain other friends. I can remember him giving me a Bible and encouraging me that this was just a terrible storm in my life and in time all would be well. He knew that even though at that time I was not a Christian, I was always thanking God and praying, not just now but from ever since I can remember. Let the truth be spoken, not in my wildest dreams did I ever guess what was to come and where I would be today.

Feeling hurt and dejected I went away to Canada for a period of time and met this lovely woman who feel head over heels in love with me. However, at that time I said that I would never trust or fall in love with another woman again. She felt the full force of my defence system which I had put up so that no woman could get a close look in. Looking back, now, although I was not horrible to her, she did not get treated in the way I should have treated such a lovely woman but that is history now. This terrible period in my life was going to take some time to get over.

One of my biggest concerns was how the break-up had affected my children, which I knew it did. My Mother and all who were close to me could see and were concerned about the pain I was going through. In addition, I lost the house which I had sweated hard for, but through all of this, my Family was there for me and, crucially, the Lord was right beside me, even though at the time I was not fully aware of it.

There were all kinds of stories going around as to what had happened to me and how I could end up, but one of the things that stood me in good fast was my fighting spirit which I would go deep and draw upon whenever the going got rough, and believe me, this was a profoundly rough time.

The illness that I mentioned earlier, that I had developed in the early 80s, before I left for Jamaica, well it had never left me and, as time went on, the numbness in my spine and left side got worse. After a long time off sick from work, the Royal Mail decided to give me retirement on medical grounds after seven years of service. Do not even think it. The pay off I got was a couple of weeks' salary – a spit in the ocean! Despite this, even though the odd dance promoters would still try to get me back on the circuit, I was not having it. There were interests in doing interviews with me but I refused. A lot of those guys who wanted to interview me did not have a clue about the business and the extent of the work I had done so how could they do a balanced interview?

As time went on, slowly I began to heal on a spiritual level. I felt then that all my life I was helping people only for my help to be thrown back in my face and for me to be used and abused. One thing that those who have done me wrong did not realize was that the blessings of God were constantly with me. But even I, myself, was not fully aware of this, either, until many years later. Thank you, Jesus.

So what was I going to do next with my life? Yes, it was time for me to open a business again, but what? The year was now 2003 and the estate where I had lived for many years, Angell Town Estate, had vacant business premises to let so I approached management with the proposals of a long time pipe-dream that I had, which was to open a mini mart/corner shop on the estate. Some people had tried to run a corner shop there before but on both occasions it did not last long. Now, as I had said before, Angell Town Estate was a place with hardcore villains – left, right, and centre.

This new wave of gang culture was also sweeping the rest of London so in order to run a business round there you had to have the respect of the local gangs. If you were a soft touch, or they did not respect you, your place of business was going to be terrorised, in some cases with proprietors having to pay out protection money. But my attitude was, 'Well, I am going to open my business and let us see who is going to try it on with me.' The prominent gang who was controlling the estate at that time was **PDC** (Poverty Driven Children or Peel Dem Crew). There was also a rival crew from the nearby Myatts Field estate, who were dubbed **Baghdad** (or Baghdad Young Ones), which was run by some Muslim youths. These two sets of gangs were somewhat terrible, to say the least. And right in the middle of this was a Yard (Jamaican) crew who at times was quite a handful themselves. Would you open a business there?

The premises where I was to open the corner shop had a tenant occupying it although his tenancy had expired and he should have vacated the premises in order for me to go in. On the morning that I was to get the keys he decided he was not moving at this time, despite the fact that I already had my equipment ready to be delivered. But nothing ever seems to run smoothly for me without a fight. The management for the premises was left with egg on their face. There was another empty unit which was a hairdressing shop so they offered this to me for temporary occupation until they completed the legal proceedings to evict the tenant from the original premises that I was to have. Knowing very little about the hair business I quickly did some research to see if this would be a viable option for me. I weighed up the situation and decided that I would open the hairdressing salon until they got this tenant out of the shop which was my original plan.

I will say it again and again; that anyone who knows me personally can testify that anything I venture to do will not be done in half measures and that presentation has to be right. Within a short space of time I turned this run down premises into a fine looking hair saloon and gave it the name **Hair We Go.** I managed to get some great stylists to work for me and the business took off. The local ladies where soon to embrace and support it and the word was getting around about this new shop. Again the haters started to surface, wanting to see me fail but the good Lord was protecting me. After what seemed like eternity they managed to evict the tenant from the shop and I took that one over as well, so instead of one, I now had two businesses. This was making the haters mad. Again I transformed the run down shop into a lovely, fully stocked, mini-mart called **Angell Town**

Corner Shop. I had the place under control and the locals were supporting it because of who I was; because I got on well with most people and they respected me.

One day I was in the corner shop and one of the top men of the local gangs came in. He started to waffle on about how one of the other local businesses who was paying them protection money said, "Why don't you also tax Uncle?" (That was what some of them started to call me). This young man was talking as if he agreed with what the other shop owner had said. I laughed and said he was watching too many dumb gangster movies and believing his own hype. What this so-called gangster did not realize was that his father and I grew up together and also that he would be playing with fire and would have gotten burnt. For some reason he quickly came to his senses and left the shop. Both shops where doing well and many did not like it, but God was protecting me.

Nevertheless, day by day my illness was getting worse. I felt so drained and tired from running both businesses so I decided to take a holiday and take my three children to Disney World in Orlando, Florida and we had a great time.

In life you never know who you will meet and what is around the corner, and destiny would have it that at this time I was going to meet my future wife, even though I had sworn not to fall in love again, or to trust another woman. After returning from holiday I met a lovely woman named **Elizabeth**, who was a cousin of one of my close friends. I knew her a little before, but not on a close basis. However, over a period of time, we started courting, although marriage was nowhere on my mind. Marriage? You would have had to be kidding.

It was now January 2006 and I was riddled with spinal pain and numbness. I could barely bend over to pick up anything and this was taking its toll on me, especially with my day to day running of the shops. The doctors said I was going to need surgery – the sooner the better, for this condition could end up crippling me. This seemed like more dark days ahead for me but, also unknown to me at the time, the greatest thing in my life was soon to happen. I had never had major surgery before so to say I was not worried would have been a great understatement.

My loving and caring wife, Elizabeth Gordon; one in a million.

By this time the relationship between Elizabeth and me was going from strength to strength and we where both aware of each other's past. She had two children, a girl and a boy, and I had a girl and two boys so we would now have five children. My dear old Mother taught me that you cannot love the cow and not the calf. She said, "Son, if you ever get involved with a woman in life and she has children before she met you and you are serious about her, you have to accept and love her children like your own and the same goes for her." My Mother opened me up to a lot of wisdom and I respected her even more, especially because she raised me single-handedly. Even though I knew of my Dad, she was the real deal.

Me and Elizabeth spoke about marriage but nothing was concrete. The hospital had now given me a date for my surgery – May 2006, but no specific day. One day I was at the shop and my phone rang. "Is that Mr Gordon.?" the voice asked. "This is King's College Hospital. We have a bed available now, can you come in tomorrow?" This was to be the most fearful and darkest day accompanied by the greatest time of my life, all rolled into one. Unknown to me, I was now going to meet and experience the Lord God ALMIGHTY through His Son, our Lord and Saviour Jesus Christ.

There were certain arrangements to be made regarding the businesses and last minute things that I had to get for I would be in the hospital for approximately three to four weeks. The day flew past and the morning came. I had not slept well and I remember all the different thoughts going through my mind. Foremost amongst them was: will the operation be successful? Would I come through this surgery ok as it was to be on my spine and that is a serious area? I can remember the sympathetic look from my daughter, Anecia, as well as the worried look on Elizabeth's face as she made sure that I had what was needed to take with me. The taxi arrived and I made my way to the hospital with members of my Family.

When I arrived they were still waiting for a bed on the ward for me so I sat in the visitors' room for quite some time. Whilst I waited I smoked some roll up, wishing it was a 'you know what'. This was going to be the last time I would smoke in my life. The nurse finally called me and showed me to my bed. Again, what was going to happen to me I could never have imagined. I was going into theatre the next day and the operation would last about five to six hours. I asked God if only it could be a success, and then this pain that I had been suffering with for the past twenty five years would be a thing of the past. But that was only wishful thinking.

The time had come and they wheeled me done to theatre. Elizabeth was holding my hand and kept on saying, "You will be alright." My youngest son, Shamar, was there looking bewildered. "Don't worry, son, everything is going to be alright," I said. The surgery went on for nearly six hours and then they brought me out and into the HDU (high dependency unit) for recovery. After several hours I came round but was still very much sedated. I remembered seeing what looked like Elizabeth's face but I could not be sure. It took a long time for me to fully recover from sedation, and then my head felt as if it was going to explode.

It was apparent that something went wrong during the operation but the doctors were not letting on. Two days had past, going into three, and my head was getting worse. After consultation by the surgeons they decided that they had to open me up again! This time they were going to fit a plastic tube called a **cerebral shunt** to drain excess fluid from the lower right part of my brain (which they believed to be the cause of the terrible pain in my head). From my brain, the tube would drain into my stomach and would remain within me for the rest of my life.

If I thought that was the last of it, I was so wrong. After this second operation it took about a week for my head to calm down and I could not walk without total assistance for I had no feelings in my spine. Elizabeth would be rushing back and forth between her jobs to visit me and to make sure I wasn't in need of anything that was within her powers. This woman was really caring for me with a genuine love. After nearly 4 weeks I came out of hospital but I was not a pretty sight

– I had suffered a considerable amount of weight loss. At this time something struck my heart and even though I had totally ruled out marriage it was plain to see that Elizabeth would make a first class wife. All of my Family liked her, especially my Mum. She could see after what happened with my children's mother that this woman was different. I decided we would get married sooner rather than later so we set a date for the 29th July 2006. This was going to be the most memorable day of my life for reasons no one could ever have imagined.

I was still nowhere fully recovered, and my illness was only minutely improved, but we started organising the wedding. This is why I have called this book *From One Extreme to Another*. Look what was going to happen now. The wedding was then just three days away, but I noticed that anything I ate or drank, regardless of how little it was, I could hardly swallow it! Even though my movements were limited I was still trying to help out as much as I could. And that was a big mistake. What was about to unfold brings tears to my eyes every time I remember it. What I was about to experience was going to change my life and the life of all those close to me, dramatically.

Just when I thought my life could not get any worse, here came the bat out of hell. Satan wanted to wipe me out, and this time for good. The day before the wedding (the Friday) my swallowing problem got worse. I now could not swallow at all! Decision time: what should I do? Postpone the wedding, or rush back to Accident and Emergency (A and E) at King's College Hospital? One thing was for sure, I had to stay focused as best I could. Elizabeth kept on asking me if I was well enough to proceed with the wedding for she would rather cancel the wedding than lose me. All my life I was never one to throw in the towel when the going got tough. I was in a terrible state but I was trying to conceal it the best I could. My brain was in overdrive.

In the evening, about 7.30pm, I made my way to pick up some fried fish which a friend had prepared for the wedding. Being hungry I tried to see if I could swallow a little piece of the fish. I had to spit it out, it could not go down. I was in a terrible state but I could not let anyone know. I remember praying, "Please God, help me." I kept on repeating this to myself. When I got back to my house, all eyes were on me.

Chapter 11

WEDDING DAY

It was now **Saturday 29th July 2006**. This was to be the day in my life when I was to acknowledge what I always read in the Bible about miracles. The difference was that instead of reading about it I was now going to experience the first of several miracles which would happen to me. A close friend called Evroy came to pick me up at 7.00am for we needed to make some final preparations at the venue where the reception would be kept. The first stop was to collect the drinks which were being stored at Elizabeth's cousin's house.

We would also collect some food stuff. As we drove along, Evroy asked me if I was ok. I replied, "No, I cannot swallow and my spine is also in pain." He stopped at a shop and asked me if I needed some water. I asked him for a can of ginger beer and he went to get it for me. When he came back to the car he handed me the drink, which I opened and took a small sip of. I could not swallow it, no matter how hard I tried. I was in a terrible state and Evroy could see it. He asked, "What do you want me to do? Shall I take you home?" I replied in a barely audible voice, "No, I will be alright," but to be truthful I was in trouble but I did not want to let down my wife-to-be.

After sorting out what was needed to be done at the venue, Evroy took me back to my house to get dressed for the wedding. One of my brothers and my son, Shamar, was there to help get me dressed. I had bought a white two piece suit to wear, which I was told looked great. Everyone kept asking me if I was ok and my usual reply was that I was fine. What a lie that was. The only thing on my mind was to be able to complete the wedding ceremony and I kept on praying, "God help me make it through." The weather was nice, a lovely warm day. Now that I was finally dressed, my brother, Mark, who was my driver, said, "Are you ready? Let's go, then." My dear old Mother was not going to be able to make it because of her health. She hugged me and gave me a kiss and said, "God be with you, son. Hope everything goes well." The church was not too far away so within a short space of time we were there. Some of our guests had already arrived, also my best man, which was Neville. I walked up to the front pew and took a seat. One of my other brothers asked me if I was nervous and I said no. Little did he know that my problem was bigger than pre-wedding nerves. I should explain here that not many people knew that I was getting married because if I had invited a quarter of the people I knew it would it would have needed a church like Westminster Abbey to accommodate them. So it was a big surprise to many who heard about it afterwards and some of them have never forgiven me for not telling them, but that's life.

Elizabeth was running late and some of the guests were wondering if she had ditched me! (Joke). All I kept saying to myself was, 'God, please let me make it through.' Finally the ushers said, "The bride is here," so I stood up and took my position in front of the altar and presently, the organist started playing that familiar tune. Elizabeth's cousin, Clive, was playing the role to give her away as her father was no longer alive. She walked slowly down and joined me. She looked so amazing! I knew she was worried because she knew that I was still fresh from the recent bouts of surgery but what she did not know was how bad I really was.

Now, in our wedding ceremony there was a part when we would both have to kneel for a period of time. This was going to be crucial because of my spinal condition. When the time came I knelt down with the greatest of difficulty. It was most uncomfortable for me, and when it came to standing up again, I wobbled a bit. I was hoping that no one saw. Well, no such luck. Let me introduce you to my eldest sister, Yvonne. She noticed it. Many people who knew about the break-up with my children's mother did not know that I was involved with anyone and this applied to my sister, who had just met Elizabeth during my hospital stay. I was always her favourite out of the boys and knowing what heartbreak I had been through she was very over protective and did not trust any woman for me. She could not understand why I decided to get married at this particular time and had her opinions and thoughts about my wife-to-be. The Bible tells us 'judge not', so after getting to know Elizabeth more closely, and seeing the way this woman cared for both me and our Mother, she realized that this woman was sent by God to be in my life. The rest of the ceremony went through and we were now **man and wife**.

By this time my condition was deteriorating but only God and I knew this. Our wedding contingent proceeded outside to take some photos and some of the local residents who knew me had also gathered. It looked like a celebrity couple was getting married. I had ordered a white stretch limousine, unknowingly to Elizabeth. My sister Yvonne came up to me and said, "I saw you stumble, are you sure you are alright? Why did you choose to go through with this now, and I thought you said it was a little wedding? It sure is not!" I can remember thinking, **'Please** shut up,' so I quickly diverted away from her and sighed relief.

It was time to make our way to the reception, which was a long distance from the church. Again Elizabeth kept asking me if I was sure that I am alright. Again my reply was, yes. My voice had lost quite a bit of volume and I thought, 'Will I be able to make my wedding speech? Please God, help me.' The good Lord was answering my prayers all the way. Listen to this: another close friend who was part of my Stereograph sound system crew, and who had become a Born Again Christian, said he and his wife would only be able to attend the church when I had invited them originally. However, on the day of the wedding, God spoke to their hearts and told them to attend the reception as well and to give their assistance in all areas of running it. Neither they nor I knew at this time that this was divine intervention from God and what else was to unfold.

My friend's name was **Carlton** but we use to call him Spinner and his wife's name was **Arleen**. The reception started after we took some more photos and slowly but surely I was getting worse. Both Carlton and his wife kept asking me if I was ok, because they did not like how I looked. Again, I said I was fine. It was time for us to be seated at the head table to make our speeches and have our meal.

I managed to make my groom's speech with great difficulty and divine help from God. When mealtime arrived, the caterers served both me and Elizabeth but I did not even attempt to eat mine because by this time I could barely breathe, let alone swallow. They removed my food from the table and said I should try a cup of soup, which they brought immediately. However, I knew that this was impossible. Elizabeth, I could see, was very worried but still trying to keep it together. By this time my voice had nearly gone completely, so I whispered in her ear. I told her that when we cut the cake I will not be able to swallow so she should just put a small piece in my mouth, which I will spit out once the photos had been taken.

The alarm bells started to really ring after the next round of photo taking, then cutting the cake, and doing our wedding dance, which until this day I do not know how on earth I managed to complete. Well, I do now, but not at the time. Afterwards, we both started to walk around to welcome our guests but that did not last long before I had to find a seat, fast. I was sitting behind the bar and my friend Carlton came and checked on me again. This time, however, he had this look on his face which I did not notice the numerous times before when he had asked me if I was alright.

166

I was slowly dying but I did not realize this. Friends were coming up to me, wishing me well and I could just about nod my head. Then consider that some of our guests were just arriving but some were not even in attendance as yet. Carlton and Arleen together came over to me and said that God had just spoken to them in their spirits and told them that they needed to get me to an A&E (casualty) hospital immediately. They found Elizabeth and calmly told her what they were feeling. She came and hugged me and said, "Come on, darling." I can remember slowly walking past some guests who asked me where I was going. I replied that I would not be long.

Carlton, Arleen, my best man Neville, and Elizabeth got into Carlton's car with me. Again the intervention of God directed Carlton to take me to King's College in Camberwell and not Mayday (now called Croydon University Hospital), which was just nearby. He thought it would be crucial that I went to Kings because I had recently done the surgery there and they would have a better understanding of my condition. The big question was obviously the long distance to King's and considering my rapid deterioration, could I make it in time? I was struggling to breathe by the minute and Carlton decided he was taking me to Kings and put his trust in God. Thereafter he drove like an ambulance, minus the sirens. By the time we arrived at A&E, there were only minutes to spare. We rushed in, still in our wedding suits and Elizabeth in her wedding dress. The other people who were waiting looked stunned – was this for real or were these people coming from some fancy dress party? I was slumped over the chair and Elizabeth shouted to staff, "My husband is dying!" They took one glance at me and rushed me round the back. There was total panic. I could feel the final breath going to leave my body. When they started to resuscitate me the oxygen masked was quickly placed on my face and tubes connected all over my body. The doctors said if I'd come a few seconds later I would have expired. This was also to be the first of three times within a few days that God was going to save me from certain death. The second time was less than 48 hrs after the first, so how can anyone tell me that God does not exists. Thank you, Jesus.

They sent for the surgeon who was a specialist in this field. He would be some time because he was over at St Thomas' Hospital in Waterloo. I can remember what he looked like even though I was sedated and my mind was all over the place. He was a tall, slim Black doctor. Without further delay he started a close examination of my airways which, no doubt, were now blocked. There was this expression on his face which suggested that this man is one lucky person. He took Elizabeth to one side and told her what was needed to be done to keep me alive. They would have to cut my throat open to free up my airway. Also, one of my flaps, excuse my terminology for the larynx, was stuck completely in the open position. The next major problem was that anything that went in by mouth was in danger of going straight into my lungs, which again could kill me.

Yes, this was a wedding that no one could forget. One of my wife's guests, we had later learnt, made a cruel remark after I was rushed to hospital. Elizabeth was gutted to know she could say what she had said, but that is how some people are. The rest of guests had arrived and as the reception continued they were unaware of the severity of what was going on. It was time to take me to theatre and Elizabeth had to sign the consent form. By now, my Family had gotten news of the near fatal circumstances and my youngest son at the time, Shamar, was completely distraught; his emotions were all over the place. I was later told it took a long time for them to get him to a calm state. Whilst I remained in hospital all three of my children would visit me often, but Shamar would be there every day. He had missed me really badly because at the time of my admission he was living with me. After my hospitalization, however, he later went to stay with his mother and visited me until I finally came out of hospital again.

When one of my other brothers got to the reception and heard that I was going into theatre, the news left him shell shocked. Think then how it was going to hit my dear old Mum when she heard. They had to delay telling her and when they did, they gave her none of the in-depth details. My Mother was a person who worried over the simplest of things and this news could have finished her off in her own fragile and still undiagnosed state. It was Elizabeth who went and told her eventually, and it hit her like a bomb. But this was just the beginning and part of the reason why I have titled this book, *From One Extreme to Another.*

Chapter 12

AT DEATH'S DOOR AGAIN

For four hours the surgeons operated to keep me alive. My throat was cut opened and after the operation I could not talk even if I wanted to. They put me in the HDU (high dependency unit) for observation after coming from theatre and the only person allowed to see me was Elizabeth. I really felt sorry for her. What a nightmare she underwent; she could have been a wife and a widow all on the same day. The nightmare was far from over, though, for Satan was determined to finish the job. After a long while I became fully conscious and could make out that I was in this specialist unit. The first thing I realized was that there was this long plastic tube coming from the area of my throat with branches connected to monitors all over my body. This was like what you would see in the movies.

Two nurses kept checking on me at short intervals. There was a mask over my face connected to an oxygen supply. One of the two nurses who were attending to me changed over the supply that was feeding the mask. Within seconds after she did this I felt as if every breath I took would be my last; my consciousness was leaving me and my eyes started to close. I knew that I was in further trouble but I could not call out or move to bring attention to the nurses that something was wrong. Here came God to my rescue again. Just as the last breath was leaving me and my eyes began to close, the other nurse turned around and by what could only be described as divine intervention, she hit the supply and ripped the mask off my face. "What are you doing?!" she shouted at her colleague. She quickly hooked me back up, pulled the screens round my bed, and started furiously to work on me. After a few minutes I was revived back to how I was before the change over. The nurse who made the error was stunned and kept on apologising. The rescue nurse was still fuming because I was given the wrong oxygen supply.

I could have died from what might have been termed gross negligence but this was now the second time the good Lord had spared my life within just over 24 hours. I later on found out that the nurse that saved me was a Born Again Christian and you are going to marvel when I reveal further on how this came to light. Continue to read, dear reader.

Some of my close friends who later on found out what had happened said that I should have sued the hospital for compensation. Well, listen to me, as far as I was concerned I got my compensation when God entered into the spirit of that nurse whose back was turned to me at the time and caused her to turn around and did what she did. A few days had now passed and there were a lot of loose ends to tie up but I could do nothing to assist Elizabeth. They decided to take me out of the HDU and place me on a ward. Oh, yes, I forgot to tell you that my sister brought a woman Pastor to pray for me and this same Pastor was going to play a crucial part in my life and become a spiritual mentor in my later Christian life. I was now on a ward, grateful to be alive. Yvonne, my eldest sister, was in a terrible state but it was a blessing when she brought Rev. G Beneochrist to pray for me.

As I met her it was already clear to me that this meeting was an act of God and truly a miracle. Elizabeth was feeling the same way that I was. This was the first time I was meeting the pastor and after our introductory talk, she began to pray. What I did not know was that during those first crucial hours she was already interceding for both me and Elizabeth. She said the Lord was calling me and He was there with me. It was not that she was trying to convince me, because I felt the same way. It was just confirmation through one of the Lord's servants. The time had come for me to surrender my life to the Lord and accept Him as my personal saviour. I did not have to think about it or get anyone's opinion. I just knew in my heart that this was the time and the greatest thing I was to do in my life. I confessed my sins to Him and declared my belief that He is the Son of God and invited Jesus Christ into my life. It was the same for Elizabeth; she felt the same way, and right there and then, on my hospital bed, I became a Born Again Christian, along with my wife. This was on **Monday 31st July, 2006.**

Yet again, there were more revelations to unfold. I could never have envisaged that the third time that God was going to save my life was not too far away.

The ward where I was being cared for as a specialist ward so they were clued up on the care and monitoring I needed. That would certainly be helpful for I would be going through surgery again. That would make a total of four times under the knife. The ward manager decided to move me to another ward but the problem with this was that the ward he decided to move me to was not clued up on my somewhat unusual condition. This move was going to be disastrous.

They moved me up to the third floor in the morning. I had a strange feeling going through me, apart from my existing pains. The day past quickly and Elizabeth was not pleased that they had moved me, either but there was not much I could do at the time. Visiting time came to an end and Elizabeth and Shamar left. It was now after 9.00pm and no one had checked on me for a good while. At 11.40pm my pain level had increased and I started to struggle to breathe. I did not panic at first but I was getting worse and could hear the nurses down the hallway talking, but not one came for me to draw this to their attention. I then started to press franticly on the emergency buzzer but still no help came and I could not get out of the bed, owing to my spinal surgery. I remembered thinking, 'Here I go again.' By now my breathing had literally stop and I could not raise the alarm. I felt my heart about to shut down and I thought, 'This is it, I am going to die, I am not going to make it a third time.' By now my eyes were almost closed and through my limited vision I saw a nurse coming towards the door. I did not know what she saw; all I can say is that it was God again. She rushed over without hesitation and started to resuscitate me, then queried why I did not press the buzzer. It would not have been nice, the answer she would have gotten if I was able to talk. This was God's mercy on me for a third time. I wrote a short note in the morning and it was given to the ward manager. It stated: "Move me back to where I was because if I die in this ward due to negligence my blood would be on your hands." I was moved by the afternoon, back to the ward where they had moved me from.

This whole situation was so hard for me and to me it was in no way coming to an end. I felt it was just the beginning of the downturn of my life again. But the difference now was that I had accepted Jesus Christ in my life.

It was July when I went into hospital and what I did not know was that I would not be leaving there until November. There are so many things you can learn from certain situations that will take place during your life, and I certainly learnt many from this. What will the future hold for me? Will I be able to cope with the emotional side of things? These were just two of the many life-and-death questions that I would be faced with.

The next decision the doctors made was about the **tracheostomy** (or tracheotomy) **tube** that would have to be placed in my throat to provide an airway to help me to breathe. I was already approved as 'nil by mouth'. Instead, I was being fed through a **feeding-tube** which was going through my nose and into my stomach. You do not want to know what that is like. The next major concern was, would I be able to speak again after all procedures were finished? At that time I had to write everything down. Those were dark days for me; times when I had to dig deep and trust in the Lord. The devil was playing his usual mind games, constantly trying to sow his seeds of doubt. I would make one step forward and three steps backward in progress with my illness. There are many sayings used by the old folks that one could relate to my situation, such as: "He who feels it, knows it." Before this I could only imagine what it must be like for a dumb person.

I was now in that position and let me tell you, I found it very frustrating most of the time. Not being able to eat as normal was not a walk in the park, either. Being fed through a tube it would take four hours for me to finish one sachet of liquid substitute-food. The next problem, among many, which I was faced with (and in some cases, still to this very day) was excessive trapped wind and constipation. This would leave me in terrible pain at times – unbearable when you think about it. No matter how much protein and essential vitamins this sachet of liquid food contained, it could not replace normal food and how it reacts in your body. I underwent the mental torture of feeling thirsty but not being able to drink but seeing people around me being able to. These were some of the darkest days of my life and yet still there was so much more to come.

The day arrived when the actual tracheostomy (or tracheotomy) tube was going to be fitted into the hole they had cut open in my throat. Yet again more torture. Prior to having my tracheostomy tube fitted I had never heard of or seen one before. This was going to be another life changing experience.

I remember going into theatre to have it fitted and after it was put into place, the first of many discomforts was to begin. They secured it by stitching the corners to my skin, which was to eventually tear! The feeling of this tube in my throat was more than weird. At this time I still could not speak but they told me that my voice and speech would eventually return if I was lucky. The majority of people who I have since met over the years with a tracheostomy tube in their throat cannot speak, and in a few cases, if they can speak, it is barely audible, with no clear voice. The collar which holds it in place makes a channel in your neck which, over a period of time, becomes sore. Just think what that must be like for me; I have had mine since September 2006 to this present day in 2012. When my wife does my daily change of dressing and cleaning of the hole in my throat, mere words cannot explain the feeling of relief for those few minutes that the collar is released. There are many other complications that also come with having the tracheostomy tube, but I will not go into these now for they are too distressing.

Another of the problems I would have to deal with was my difficulty with walking and balance, owing to my spinal condition for which the medical name is **Arnold Chari Malformation** (ACM). This is an obstruction of fluid flow between the brain and the spine. It is terrible, and just like the tracheostomy tube, I am still battling with stopping it from getting worse. Every day as I my life, if it was not for the good Lord I do not how I could continue. Muscle wastage is one of the attributes of ACM and it has made my left arm and hand redundant by severe deformity. In other words, I am experiencing what it is like for a person who has only one arm, even though mine is still attached to my body. A Zimmer frame was to become my rehabilitation support in my trying to walk again. What little walking ability I have today is again a miracle because this was not looking possible at one time. By no means is my walking great, though. It has to be aided by a walking stick and I often lose balance. If I fall over I cannot get up without the assistance of someone.

I do not know what the thinking of other individuals is, but I know that having my life and being able to go through it daily is because of the goodness and mercy of my Lord and Saviour Jesus Christ. Each day that I was in hospital seemed like a year. There were times when I looked forward to my visits and there were other times when I did not want to see anyone. My dear old Mother would struggle nearly every day to visit me, even though her pains and illness she was faced with were taking their toll. The love and sorrow she felt for me was always plain to see. On two occasions whilst visiting and leaving she took a fall in the street, and I thank God that on both occasions He sent a Good Samaritan to help her. These falls, however, were playing heavily on my mind. She would walk all the way to the hospital and back, and no matter how much I told her not to come she would turn up. The only way my Mother was not going to come was if she could not totally move or if I was out of the hospital.

It was now near the end of September and financial difficulties were surfacing. My businesses were both closed, having no one who could take charge. Mr Bills was not taking any prisoners. Elizabeth was working hard to make ends meet, and frustration became my middle name. I will explain again, this is why this book is named, *From One Extreme to Another.* We had not yet opened the cards and presents that we'd received from our wedding guests. Elizabeth wanted us to do this together. On one of her evening visits she brought them in and we sat on my bed and open them together. They were all lovely but two in particular just blew us away. They came from friends we did not know had such thoughts towards giving us a financial gift. One contained two hundred pounds (£200) and I will not even tell you how much was in the other! That just took care of a few bills, rather nicely. This was more blessings from God in our life again.

My condition, I now had to accept, might be for life. I was plagued by several detritions; my spine was in a severe condition, I suffered from blockage of my airways and my loss of mobility due to muscle wastage. On top of all this, where were we going to live – me, Elizabeth and Shamar? At the time of going into hospital, I was in the middle of sorting this out but it was not completed, so we would have to stay at my Mother's place. The problem with this was the lack of space.

This situation left me feeling personally degraded because I was always used to sorting out whatever it was I was faced with, but the big hindrance now was my physical condition. I could just about stand up let alone move around. And the fact that I might not regain my voice was soul destroying. I remember thinking, 'God, can this get any worse?' Well, you know what? It did. But I had to start learning to trust the good Lord even more; I had to have more faith. After speaking with the consultant and care team, they got this notion that I might be sinking into serious depression. I do not know what they saw but I knew that it was not so. The next thing I knew they took the decision to assign a psychologist to me. We had a few meetings and it ended up that I was counselling him. This rollercoaster ride was far from over.

It was the start of October 2006 and there was still no clear indication of how much more time I would have to spend in hospital. They had now fitted a replacement feeding tube, called a PEG[6] tube, directly into my stomach. Whereas I was fed previously through the tube which went through my nose and into my stomach, this one was now direct into my stomach and if I was feeding and wanted to go to the toilet I would have to wheel the stand with the feed on it with me. Many times I was so fed up that I would stop the feed and try to have a little walk to clear my head. The problem with that was that the four hours that the feed would previously take would now take even longer. Also, the back of my hands and arms were so sore from the amount of drips and blood tests they had been taking I did not know how much more I could take.

One night I had a terrible reaction to the drugs. My arm on which the drip was connected had swollen like a balloon, plus my airways became blocked and I was trembling so uncontrollably I felt horribly like I was going to die again. Elizabeth, my wife, refused to leave me

---

[6] percutaneous endoscopic gastrostomy

and go home. She stayed all night and was also joined by a close friend. It was touch and go. The tears were rolling down my face and I could not hide my sadness but I managed, with difficulty, to position my face so that Elizabeth and our friend could not see me. I knew that as strong as she was, if she had seen me weeping this would have made her break down.

I was not one for large amount of friends visiting me in hospital but there were some who I thought were close but I did not see them even once in the entire four months I was there. Then there were those who were known to have made some hypocritical and unkind comments about me. This was to be another refresher lesson about the behaviour of some people who call themselves your friends. But this was all part of the preparation that God was putting me through, even up to this day.

All of my children felt sad at what was happening but the one it hit the hardest was the youngest at the time, Shamar. Since the split between his mother and me, he had been living with me most of the time and we went through some tough emotional times. I could see how lost he was when he visited me in hospital, which was mostly every day. He was 14 years old at the time and he used to help me run the corner shop business. He was my right hand man and was gifted with a head for figures. It was particularly hard on him when visiting time was over, knowing that he had to leave me.

The question that I kept asking myself was how I would cope with life knowing that I would not be able to do any physical work again; being unable to perform the majority of everyday tasks. It was only going to be a short while before I started to get the answers. Another agonising point for me was seeing patients who were admitted after me having their surgeries done and being discharged while I still remained on the ward. Financial pressure was continuously mounting and serious decisions had to be made by this time. It was apparent that I would have to close both businesses to clear up certain debts that had been incurred. This was not an ideal situation to be in with my medical condition. To be mentally stressed would greatly hinder any little progress that could be made in my circumstance. My Family or the odd friend would visit me, but more often than not, it was burdensome for Elizabeth who would keep on encouraging me on a spiritual level; out of everyone, she knew the emotional and financial turmoil we were both going through.

There was a considerable amount of cash owed to me by various persons and I tried to recover the money but because I was in hospital they took full advantage of this not to pay. These were people I had loaned money when they were in financial difficulties. One of these persons had purchased some equipment from me which I did not really want to sell but they constantly begged me until I agreed. When I approach this individual about my money from within the hospital he threatened me with violence. I tell you this, he was lucky that I had given my life to the Lord because even though I was ill in hospital something could easily have been arranged. My situation was like a tennis game. I was being hit back and forth and the only one I could turn to for solution was God.

The recovery treatment I was getting physically, such as physiotherapy and speech therapy, were very slow and it was now approaching the third week in October. The social care team was due to have a meeting with the surgeon and the doctors whose care I was under, to look at the possibility of me being discharged in the coming weeks. There were major issues to consider because there were so many provisions that would have to be made before I could be responsibly sent home. I would need daily visits from the district nurse to continue to administer treatment to me, and there were certain medical equipment that would have to be placed in my home. Another critical factor was the suitability of my Mother's home where I would be staying. Remember, I was in the midst of sorting out a home for us to live when all of my illnesses came to a head. The point was, if all these issues were not sorted out I was not going to be discharged because they could not take any chances with my condition.

My Mother's own condition became a major concern to me, also. Her own health had gotten worse so she could not visit me any more. That in turn was worrying her tremendously, even though I would make brief phone calls to her – I could not talk for long because of my voice. My wife would also give her a daily update on my condition, but this was not enough for Mum, who loved all of her children, but I was the apple of her eye. In her latter days she depended on me for virtually everything, apart from her financial wellbeing, for she was a very independent woman.

At nights I would not sleep. I would just lay there thinking because there was no comfortable position that my medical condition afforded me, and this is the same to this present time. You would have to be me or have a similar illness to understand what I am saying. My constant pain has been my life for the past 32 years, yes, 32 years to date, since I was 22 years of age. It is hard for me to explain to the doctors and others about the several pains I am feeling. The pains in my spine and joints have their own feelings, but that in my body is another. The nearest I could come to a description of that is this: deep within the tissues of my left side – my arm, hand, and leg, it feels like being burnt by boiling hot water and suffering that terrible burning and smarting sensation, non-stop all these years. This problem is increasingly overtaking my right side, also. In addition to my body pain, another of my disabilities is the loss of sensation in most areas of my body – yes, complete numbness whereby if you were to pinch me with the greatest force I would not know. This is so bad that often I burn myself from the cooker or the oven and I do not know it because I cannot feel it. This, in itself, is another of my many pains but this one is more mental.

There are so many reasons why I was led by God to write this book. If I can help to encourage one person to come to know the Lord Jesus Christ, or to learn how to forgive those who have hurt them, or to persevere on certain goals they would like to achieve in life, and to have Love in their heart, then it will have been worth it. The first point I have mentioned is the most important, but if they can embrace any of the others it will be a job well done.

Chapter 13

EITHER OR NEITHER

The meeting had taken place about me being discharged and the wait for the decision from the hospital was pure torment. Finally, a member of the social care team came to see me and said hopefully I should be out in the next one to two weeks, depending on my medical condition and certain provisions being in place. Immediately, the first thing that came to my mind was that things were not going to be as they were and at this point I still could not swallow so I was still being fed liquid food through the PEG line in my stomach.

The ideal situation regarding accommodation would have been for me to have my own new place but this was not to be so, therefore, for the meantime it would be back to Mum's. This was cool in the sense that I would be in a more familiar environment, but in view of my condition it was not, because of the extra work it would cost. The double operation alongside the first two had taken their toll on my physical appearance; there was no hiding the fact I did not look good. I could not even bath myself and I needed assistance in most things, thereby returning to the baby state all over again.

During my time in the hospital I was a firm favourite with most of the nurses but as you know, there will always be one and this one was straight out of Hell. Everything was a problem for her and I dreaded it when she was on duty, especially at nights. I used to call her 'worse', not nurse but she did not know this. This was one of the signs that made it evident that I was changing regarding certain attitudes and that my tolerance level had increased.

The surgeon who had performed my surgery came to see me. He highlighted the restrictions that I was going to face and told me that I would not recover fully from my condition, and furthermore that it would deteriorate over time. What he had told me did not really surprise me but nevertheless, it was a hard thing to accept but I had to face it. I sat quietly after speaking with him, just thinking the whole thing over. I told myself that this was how my life had been up until then; I have always had to face major upheavals but the good Lord has always brought me through. When Elizabeth visited I did not give her the sordid details and she knew more or less anyway what I would be faced with. The crucial factor was that she would have to cope with this situation as my wife.

The day that I had been waiting for finally arrived. This was my day to leave the hospital, though it was not the ideal situation from the domestic point of view. The amount of medical supplies and equipment which I had to take with me needed a large estate vehicle to carry it to my Mother's house. After final checks had been made on me before I left, Elizabeth and I thanked the ward staff for looking after me all this time. There were also a couple of patients who I had gotten on with quite well so I bid them goodbye. I could barely walk and had to use a Zimmer frame to support myself. Each step felt like I would not be able to take the other.

At last I was home from the wedding – must be the longest wedding observance ever! It was the start of November and my birthday was fast approaching on the 15th. This birthday was surely going to be different, but the greatest thing of all was that I was alive. I was never one for making a big fuss about my birthday and it was not going to change now.

There were to be many dark days still ahead to encounter, but one unforgettable and remarkable experience I had and was still mindful of was how I felt spiritually speaking. Since I accepted Jesus Christ as my Saviour it was like a heavy burden had been lifted from me and I had this inner peace within my spirit. What I did not know was that this was just the beginning of many miracles and pleasant things to unfold in my life. I was very appreciative of the district nurses assigned to visit me daily to apply fresh dressing to my surgery wounds. Some of them were fine, others were not. The days would seem to go fast but the nights really dragged on. What was I going to do in my life? Both of my businesses had folded up and I would need some kind of income. There was some form of financial help I could get in the form of benefits from the government but to be truthful that was never me. And in any case, I would not appreciate the amount of red tape one would have to go through only to be told you are not eligible.

It was now the start of 2007 and I was glad to see the back of 2006. By now I could walk a little better, which was great, considering that at one stage it was unsure whether I might walk again. I was still observing 'nil by mouth' on this dreaded sachet feed and my voice was showing some improvement. One night as I was lying down on my back, which was the only position I could do, an incredible thing happened. My eyes were closed but I was not into a deep sleep. Then I clearly heard this softly spoken voice say, "Get up and get a pen and paper. I want you to write for me." I thought to myself that I was imagining this so I did not respond at first. However, after my initial delay, it was if I was being assisted to get up and I did so in total amazement. I took the pen in my right hand and started to write. This is what was written down:

WHOSOEVER HEARS THE WORDS OF THE LORD AND TAKES COUNSEL ACCORDIINGLY WILL HAVE MADE A WISE CHOICE BECAUSE A STRONG FOUNDATION IS ABLE TO WITHSTAND THE ATTACKS OF DESTRUCTIVE ELEMENTS.

BE NOT LIKE THEM WHOSE EARS HAVE BEEN IMPAIRED
AND HEAR NOT DUE TO THE VOICE OF VANITY AND
INFLUENNCE OF THE WICKED FOR THEIR EYES ARE ALSO
COVERED WITH A VEIL SUPPLIED BY FORCES WHICH ARE
UNGODLY, SO SHALL THEIR VISION BE LIMITED.

REFUSE NOT TO DO WHAT CAN BE DONE TODAY BE IT
INSTRUCTED BY THE LORD.

MANY SAY THAT THEY WILL CHANGE THEIR WAYS BUT
NOT UNTIL SEVERAL MORE DANCES WITH THE ENEMY.

OH WHAT AN UNWISE DECISION, FOR TEARS OF SORROW
SHALL BE THEIR CRY.

I was in total amazement because it was as if my hands and spirit were
being led by some unknown force. This, I believe, was my first
encounter with the Holy Spirit. I was not a writer before. I just wrote
the odd letter so to pen something in depth like this had to be of the
Lord. I sat there just trying to absorb what had just taken place and
this was to be the first of many encounters of this kind. I have so many
writings and messages to preach it is beyond belief but it is not by my
strength or intelligence; it is by the awesome power of Jesus Christ,
which things He can do when you truly accept Him into your life.

I went back for the first of many checks and in March 2007 they
decided that the PEG from my stomach could be removed. After scans
and x-rays the specialist team which I was under said that one of the
flaps of my voice box was still jammed in the open position, which is
dangerous. However, they believed that I could start taking liquidised
food and some fluid by mouth – but under the strictest supervision and
extreme care. I prayed every day and asked God to make it possible
that I would be able to eat and drink as normal some day, although I
was still very limited to my intake by mouth. He was surely answering
my prayers step by step. The doctors made it known to me that there

was no way at this time that the tracheostomy tube could be removed from my throat because I would be in a life threatening situation.

My first sip of drink was pure bliss and moments like that I could not forget. By this time my voice was getting stronger and clearer. The doctors again were amazed; if my tube was covered you could not tell that I was a tracheostomy patient. The majority of other people who I was now meeting more frequently who had this tube in their throats could not speak and if they did it was not audible or clear. What was evident to me was that miracles were again manifesting right before me in my life. My walking had also improved but I had to be aided by a walking stick. And even now, because of the nature of my spinal condition, my balance is not good and if I were to fall over, which has happened from time to time, I could not get up on my own.

Your mental state of mind when you are faced with lifelong illnesses which gradually get worse can be a real see-saw. There are days when you cope brilliantly and there are others when you just want to fold up in some corner. But what has kept, and is keeping me strong is my faith and trust in the Lord. The next thing on my and Elizabeth's full agenda was to find a church to join. We had already become Born Again Christians but we needed a church in the congregational sense, which as a true believing Christian you must do. We visited a few but did not feel that they were where we should be.

My friend who'd stayed overnight in the hospital with me and Elizabeth, when I had that attack, invited us to a church in the Battersea area of south London, a Church of God of Prophecy Pentecostal denomination. She herself was a Christian but was not a member of the church but a member of the Methodist church which shared the building with the one she invited us to. I remember the first Sunday we walked into this church, not knowing anyone apart from our friend who had invited us there. The initial feeling I got was warm, and a couple of members greeted us. Later on we found out that one of the ministers was someone I knew from my sound days when she used to attend the dances before giving her life to the Lord.

Talk about 'from one extreme to another', here I was now seeking to serve the Lord and gone were the days of my hardcore life under the influences of Satan. This was and still is making the devil mad. Another one of his key workers repented of his ways and does not intend to look back. It is all out war! Again what was going to unfold? I could not imagine what the Lord had in store for me.

May 2007 saw more miracles manifesting again in my life. A manager from the social care team arranged to visit me. They were fully aware of my housing situation and informed me that because of my urgent medical condition they would need to house me as soon as possible in suitable accommodation for myself, Elizabeth and Shamar. I had a friend named Derek who I had known for many years. He worked in the housing department and he called me up one day to see how I was. Whilst speaking with him the topic came up about my housing situation and he gave me some vital contact information and guidance on what to pursue. In my search I met this housing manager who took up my case said, "There is something special about you and I am going out, all guns blazing, to get you housed." Within a matter of a few weeks they offered me a brand new two bedroom flat in a brand new building where I was the first tenant to move in.

Now listen to this. Remember I told you that because of my Mother's worsening illness she was heavily and increasingly reliant on me? I did not want to move too far from her so that I could still keep a close eye on her, and when she knew that I would be seeking a place, she started to worry that I would be far away from her. Well, the flat that they offered me was just a stone's throw from her house! When she heard this she was so relived, and so was I. Another miracle had happened again.

Another blessing occurred for us when Elizabeth and I had our official baptism on 28 January, 2008. Thank you, Father. In furtherance of the zeal within me, and unknown to anyone, even to Elizabeth, I started to do a home correspondence course in Bible studies with KNEE University and WEBC Overseas, and I attended THG Evangelist College for ministerial training. Each day that went by it became crystal clear what my calling was and what the Lord wanted me to do.

One Sunday a visiting speaker came to our church to do the youth service. Again, this was going to have an unexpected twist in my journey. The visiting speaker preached a stirring sermon which I could instantly connect with. I did not realize at first but this was a man who knew my history but did not know that I had become Born Again. He was a man who had turned his life around from the street culture and drugs. After the service I went up to commend him and instantly he recognized me. He was amazed to see my transformation and we started to talk. I gave him part of my testimony about how I got saved. Straight away he said, "My brother, the Lord has a special anointing on you and with a testimony like yours you cannot sit down in one place; people need to hear this." I became interested in what he was saying and he continued, "There are many believers who do not realize the fact that God is still doing miracles in this very time and I need you to come to my church where I attend." This church was a branch of the one which I first become a member of. The minister's name was Brother Nicky and he was also the brother-in-law of my pastor at that time.

He invited me to come and testify at his church and this was to be the start of my preaching ministry and further amazing revelations and miracles. A date was set for me to share my first testimony with a congregation. Not even my church, where I had been attending for some considerable time, had heard the fullness of my testimony. You see, the good Lord moves in mysterious ways which we can never understand because it goes completely to the opposite of our human thinking. The Sunday morning of my testimony arrived and I was not to know what was going to take place. The church had a large congregation and the service started with praise and worship after which I was introduced. The further I went on with my testimony, the more one could see that everyone was deeply touched. By the time I had got half way through it, many eyes were filled with tears. This was the part which was going to blow me away: remember I told you about the nurse who had saved me from death the second time; who do you think was to stand up in the congregation and confirm what I had just stated but **the very same nurse!** I did not know that she was a member of that church but here was a credible witness to testify that I was not making this up. God wanted them to know.

I was moved to see how awesome the Lord is and nearly every time after that wherever I would be invited to speak there would be someone who could testify to what I was saying. Amazing! I had not planned to remove my tracheostomy tube during the testimony, I was only going to show them but then the Lord spoke to me in my spirit as I testified. He told me to remove my tube because, "There are a lot of doubting Thomases in here." When my tube is removed I have no voice and when I replace it my voice returns. When I did as the Lord told me, the whole congregation erupted, giving praises unto God. I was overfilled with emotion and tears were running from my eyes.

This was just the start of what was and is to come. One sister came over to me, amongst the many, and said that she use to complain often about her illness. However, after what she witnessed and heard that day, she undertook not to complain anymore because my illness and what I had been through made her seem like she only had a cold. A group of youths also came to me and said how blessed and inspired they were. Glory be to God.

The next plan God had for me was, again, going to blow me away. There was a church that I would often go past, and every time I did I felt in my spirit that I should go in and speak to the pastor in charge, to explain what God had done for me and see if I would be allowed to give my testimony in their church. The problem was that every time I attempted to do this it was closed, and this went on for months. This was resting heavily on my mind.

One Sunday after service at my church I decided to pay this church a visit. On entering I realized that some brothers I had known were to call the two pastors Mum and Dad, and also that I knew the deacon. I told them what was pressed in my spirit and they invited me to give the testimony. When they heard it they told me that a testimony like this needed to be heard all over. They had a telecast coming up on the gospel television channel and asked me if I would please come and be televised. Let me put the record straight before I go any further. This was not about me becoming known, or popular. It was about giving God the glory for it belongs to Him and Him alone. I was just the vessel He was using and I was honoured and felt privileged that the Lord was using me in this way for I am passionate about helping to win lost souls for the Kingdom.

The testimony got a massive response from all who had seen it on the television, so much so that it was televised for three months. The ministry which did the telecast was St Marks, pastured by Dr. Samuels whose son, Roger Samuels, is a well known gospel singer. He has been a true inspiration to me and from the first time I met him he said that he could see the anointing of the Lord on me and that God was going to use me to do great things. I was now going all over to share this wonderful testimony and starting to preach often.

I also went to do a course in mentoring, which I initially thought I would not pass but I got my qualification with flying colours. Now I was also a qualified mentor. When God is for you who can be against you? Would you like to hear of more real miracles? Please read on.

When I first met Elizabeth she had two children – a girl and a boy. I had a girl and two boys so we now had five children. Well, as you must have realized, we did not have any together for the doctors thought that with my condition there was not much chance of that happening. Nevertheless, we would often speak about how nice it would be for us to have a child together. Well, a miracle manifested again for us on the **9th of December 2008** at 11.45am when the Lord blessed us with the birth of a son, **Joel Lamon Gordon.** Thank you, again, Jesus. When the surgeon who had operated on me heard this he nearly needed surgery himself (smile), and some of the ladies joked that they were staying far away from me! The popular saying, 'never judge a book by its cover' is obviously, true.

In life you have to be able to face not only the good times but also the bad times, especially when you are in the midst of a raging storm. When you are a lukewarm Christian, or unsaved, not to say you want to be attacked by devil but he is not really bothered, just as the word of God tells us in Revelation 3:16 – the Lord cannot use you when you are lukewarm, neither hot nor cold. However, when you are on fire for the Lord you can better stand firm and fight the good fight of faith. Satan was mad that he did not get to take me out completely in 2006 and here I am now, a servant of the Lord. The word of God is controversial and if you are not willing to be challenged by it, well you are living in denial.

One day in 2009 I received a call from a man named Calvin who was a mentor to me. I knew Calvin from since my time on Soferno-B and I grew up respecting him to this day. He telephoned me and said, "Youth," (that's what he always called me, even to this day) "Do you still have any of your old selections for I know some sound men from Japan who want to buy the old revival tunes." Now, the amount of records and dub plates I've had over the years, when I was in the business, if I had all of them still I would need two houses to hold them. Over the years I've lost, through theft and unreturned loans, an uncountable amount of irreplaceable records totalling thousands and thousands of pounds. Nevertheless, I still had a large and valuable selection – some real gems. In these times you have some so-called record collectors, hungry to buy the vintage stuff and, in some cases, willing to pay top money. Anyway I said yes to Calvin and he said if I wanted he could bring them to me to do some business. At the time this would have been great as I was low on cash. But God always provides a way for His people. Now, when Calvin brought them over I told them that the only reason I would sell them some records was because they came from Japan and they told me that they wanted them for their sound.

Over the years quite a few people have approached me wanting tunes – usually sound men in England and record collectors. The sound men do not want to pay; they are looking for freebies, and the collectors I met were talking peanuts, so I did not sell any, plus I did not want my selection being played in the UK. When the Japanese saw some of my selections their eyes lit up for they knew their tunes. I also told them the only reason I would do business with them was because Calvin had referred them to me, otherwise, no way. I sorted out a selection for them and they acted like the cat that got the cream. They must have thought that I was a fool until they realized that certain of my tunes were ones that no one else could find and not be available for sale, no matter how big their money was. Only one sound man alone could get certain tunes from me and that is my bredrin **TGO Superclick**. Big up your sound, respect due. Whenever Superclick is playing against certain sounds I will happily give him old-school tunes from 'Graph' days to do his business.

Deceit had entered my life again through these Japanese. It turned out that they did not want these tunes for their sound but were sellers with an internet site selling back the tunes at big prices. Calvin, just like me, was not aware what these cunning Japanese men were doing.

I did not even find this out until quite some time later, when a French journalist who had been trying to track me down for some time finally found me. He was a big Stereograph fan and he wanted to make a documentary about Soferno-B and Stereograph. He told me he had bought most of the selection off the site and when he told me how much he paid, I nearly passed out. These two Japanese con artists' names are Matuka and Tomiah from **Rising Sun Records**. Now as you are reading about my life you can see that I have always been dealt with unfairly, but they can't stop me. By the way, I have forgiven them. My friend Calvin, I must give the most respect to him. He has been like a real father figure in my life over the years and we are still in regular contact. He always said he saw the potential of greatness in me. My regards, also, to his lovely wife, Sister Evee who is a Born Again like myself and has been an inspiration to me along my journey. God bless you both.

Another year had gone by, and by the Grace and mercy of the Lord, I am still here giving thanks and praise to be alive and slowly learning from the guidance of the Holy Spirit each day. I could sense it that 2010 was going to be a year of great significance. The Lord was telling me that it would soon be time for me to move on as I had gone through my learning process up to that point. At first in the early stages of hearing this I just dismissed it, thinking I might not have heard right; and in any case I was hoping the anointing that was on me could be use to a greater advantage at the church where I was already. I was also taking into consideration my wife and children. If it was time to move on I did not want to feel I was forcing her to follow me; it had to be from her own decision and the leading of the Spirit.

This was going to be a real battle between the Spirit and the flesh, which always takes place in the believer's life. It was the start of August and my Mother's illness had gotten worse and deteriorating fast. I was the one who took her to all her hospital appointments, even though I was under pressure myself with my illness. But here came the rollercoaster ride again. The regional overseer for the Church of God of Prophecy, who was the minister who carried out my baptism, had invited me to speak at our regional convention. Prior to this I had accepted his request for me to speak and share my testimony at the church where he was pastor and they were so touched. He had also heard me speak one Sunday at my church and was greatly blessed. He had told me that he could see the anointing on me and was the first person to give me a financial offering to my ministry. Despite the high post he held he personally took an interest in me. Thank you, Bishop Len Rowe. God bless you.

The guest speaker at the convention was Rev. L Woodstock who pastured a church in Walsall, Birmingham. I spoke just before she went on and after I came down she said to me, "I need to see you afterwards." After she had finish delivering the Word she told me that she was deeply moved and blessed by my testimony and told me that it was as good as a sermon. The Reverend then invited me to her church as the main speaker at their forthcoming crusade. She promised to structure the crusade around me, saying the Holy Spirit had instructed her to do so. She contacted me and made final arrangements for the date again. What was going to take place I could not have imagined.

Rev. Woodstock gave me the theme so that I could prepare the message I was going to deliver with my testimony. Now here came the stumbling blocks which the devil planned to use to prevent me from going. Owing to the distance and my disability, I had arranged with Brother Nicky to be my driver. (You remember, Brother Nicky was the visiting speaker who first gave me the opportunity to testify). Two days before the crusade, he had to pull out. At this time my Mother was admitted to the hospital in a serious condition on Sunday 12th September, 2010. Allow me to share something with you about the wonderful woman God had placed in my life, my wife Elizabeth. Not only was she taking care of me but she would also attend to my

Mother's needs as if it were her own mother. And I do not mean on the odd occasion, but all the time. God bless her.

My Mother had been diagnosed with serious bowel cancer which was so advanced that nothing could really be done about it. During her time in hospital, which lasted about 4 weeks, if a day went pass and she did not see me she would go to pieces, so every day I had to make sure I was there. So now that I had to go to Walsall my Mother is dying and my driver was unable to drive me to the crusade and the church is expecting me. What was I going to do? Well, there was only one answer – seek the Lord for divine guidance and favour. Where the driving was concerned, I could drive but with my medical condition this would be with the greatest of difficulty because of the distance, which was about 120 miles one way. But my main concern was my Mother. I would be away for two days because I was also booked to preach at Bishop Newland's church on the Sunday. Of course, Mum would start to worry excessively if I told her I was going and she would not see me for two days.

I remember I took up the battle position on my knees and asked the Lord to both give me the strength to drive, and to keep my Mother alive until I got back from Walsall. This was where total trust and obedience to the Lord was going to have to be fully applied. Saturday morning arrived and I, Elizabeth and two of our sons headed out for Walsall. I had to stop a couple of times to stretch my spine and get my circulation going before continuing our journey. After about four hours we arrived at Walsall and booked into the hotel where we were staying. Thank you, Jesus. The crusade was due to start at 6.00pm so we just had a couple of hours to rest and have something to eat. The church was a fair size and it was not long before every seat was taken. The moderator commenced the service and soon, when it was my time, the Rev. Woodstock introduced me to the congregation.

I started to deliver my message and then I went into the testimony. You could hear a pin drop as the congregation listened intensely. I remember seeing one woman break down in tears and it was not long before several others followed. When I removed the tube from my throat the church erupted, giving God praises. I made an altar call for the unsaved and those in need of prayer to come up. The altar was full, glory be to God. After the service had finished I was sitting on the rostrum reflecting on the awesomeness of God. With my head bowed I heard a voice say, "God bless you, minister. You do not know what you have just done." He had tears coming down his face. I immediately told him that it was not me but the Lord, but he replied, "Yes, I know, but He has used you to do it." What was to proceed out of this young man's mouth was to leave me dumbstruck and will stay with me for the rest of my earthly life. He said he was going to kill a man with the gun he had on him but when he heard my message and testimony he went and put the gun away and came and thanked me. He asked me to pray for him and gave me his telephone number, which I called on a couple of occasions to see how he was doing.

God had taken me all the way from London to minister to this young man's heart. Another woman told me that she was saved but now she was really saved for such was how she received the word of God which I had delivered. Rev. Woodstock was more than pleased and we gave God the glory.

The next day was to be the same at Bishop Newland's church. People came away feeling highly blessed. It was then time to head back to London – no time to tarry as my Mother would now be worrying because she had not seen me since Friday. I went straight to the hospital and I could see the relief on her depressed face. It just lit up as soon as she saw me. My big sister, who was there before me, told me that she would not speak before I came. I had been obedient in doing the Lord's will and He kept my Mother just as I asked him to do. They moved my Mother into a care home because she was too ill to return home but this was divine favour again from God. Normally, someone in the condition of my Mother, who had a terminal illness and did not have long to live, would be placed in a hospice, not a care home where, in most cases the environment is not very nice. However my Mother was placed in a care home where she could pass away with dignity. Here came more blessings again. My Mother was always a God fearing person who knew hymns and scriptures from the Bible more than some who were saved. But she was not a Born Again. She lived to see me become a Christian serving the Lord and I was able to minister to her in her last days before she was admitted into hospital. The greatest thing was that she confessed her sins and accepted Jesus Christ as her Saviour before He called her home. That was the greatest thing of all; she did not die a lost soul. I thank you, Jesus. My Mother passed away peacefully, in her sleep, on the 8th November, 2010.

This book is called *From One Extreme to Another* and my extreme experiences were not yet over – not by a long shot. It was now 2011 and the Holy Spirit came back to me again. The Lord was moving me on, but would I be obedient to my calling? This was a spiritually tense time for me, and where He was moving me to was into the wilderness, to prepare me further. I did not know much more than that but I knew I had to have trust and faith in Him. I waited until the Lord told me that it was the right time to tell my wife that I was leaving Battersea Church of God of Prophecy. I knew that she would not be able to fully understand, even though she was in the faith; no disrespect, but this is how it goes. When I told her it hit her hard. She felt all kinds of emotions. After explaining what the Lord was doing with me, the first thing I emphasised to her was the fact that I would dearly love her to come with me but I would not be doing or saying anything to persuade her – she would have to feel it for herself. For a time there was tension in the home. Another factor that was difficult for her to understand, perhaps the most difficult, was the fact that the ministry where I was going had nothing or no one except the pastor, his family, and me: the new ministry in the wilderness. My next move was to honour my existing pastor and tell him of my intention. He said he respected the fact that I came to him and showed him what I was doing, but I do not know what he really felt. God bless him and I love him just the same.

I was not going to make a song and dance about my leaving, so I left without any announcement or malice as far as I was concerned. Some of the other bredrin then heard and they had mixed opinions. One thing was certain, though. As far I was concerned, they could always call on me, even now that I am not there – but my wife decided to stay. My maturity had taught me that I did not come to serve man and it is better to please God than man. You have to put the Lord first above everything, regardless of what.

Near five months down the road came another crushing blow. My Dad was not in good health and was slowly diminishing. It was now **April the 3rd, 2011**, Mother's Day Sunday so I decided to go and visit Mum's grave and then go to church afterwards. Whilst I was standing at Mum's grave I had a feeling come over my spirit that I had never experienced before. When I'd finished visiting I drove back home. When I got in the house Elizabeth asked me how it went, meaning at Mum's graveside. Then I noticed this look on her face: she took a deep breath and paused, but before she could come out with what she was going to say, I felt it in my spirit. She continued, "I have some bad news for you. Your Dad just passed away." So, in less than five months after losing my Mother I had lost my Dad, also. And I had another funeral to officiate over. I was numb. At this time his body was still at his home. I sat down for five minutes to reflect on what was going on, then I got in the car and made my way round to his house. When I got there, a police car was outside with two officers. I declared who I was and made my way into the house. One of my older brothers and sister was in the house and my Dad's body was lying on the floor. He had died in my brother, Danny's arms.

Dad was a member of that famous childhood church I mentioned earlier, yes, Railton Road Methodist. However, as far as I knew, even though he was an active member in the church, he had not fully given his life to the Lord and he certainly had not been baptised. The sadness filled my heart even more. I helped to arrange and officiate at my Dad's funeral, taking the lead as the only saved one of the Family. People were saying they did not know how I coped and stayed so strong but it was the strength of the Lord sustaining me.

Keep the name of this book in mind, for the one extreme to another roller coaster continued. I was invited to speak at an ordination ceremony, and my own ordination as a minister was to follow shortly. Bishop Baxter from Canada, who was ordaining these ministers, heard my testimony and invited me to speak at his church at their annual convention. However, I had other engagements so I could not attend, but I will be going to Canada in the future.

In June 2011 I was ordained as a minister. Again I did not make a big fuss – I just went humbly and had my ordination. My Mother had two more sisters; one had died in 1981 and Mum died 2010. That left the youngest of the three sisters, my Auntie Zur. She lived in Bedfordshire and did not have any children. Her husband, my uncle, Jim, had died 8 years ago so she lived on her own. My auntie loved ambitious people so I was her favourite nephew. She admired my fighting spirit and my never-say-die attitude. Auntie Zur was in the nursing profession all her life, eventually finishing her working career as a health visitor before her retirement. In the later years, ill health plagued her and made her less and less mobile. It hit her hard when her only remaining sister, my Mother, died, for they were very close. We would speak regularly on the phone because we were her only family. She was proud of all I had achieved, the icing on the cake for her being when I gained my qualification for mentoring and my ordination as a minister, especially since she was a devoted member of her local Baptist church for many years. She told everyone about her nephew Michael. She was again in marvel of me for the way I organised and conducted my Mother's funeral, giving of my best at all times. She went back to Bedford and told everyone.

One day in the last week in August 2011, she told me she wanted to see me sooner than later. I told her I would be down shortly. Again, something in my spirit was telling me not to delay. It was two weeks into September and I was not feeling great, which more often than not is the case because, I will remind you, I am in constant pain with my illness. I, Elizabeth, and the two boys made our way up to Bedford and reached there about mid day. Auntie Zur was so glad to see us. We had lunch and she started to speak to me about personal things which she had never done before.

The line of conversation was a little uncomfortable in the sense that she was saying things like, if I die make sure you do this and do that. I told her, "Auntie, by the grace of God you are not going anywhere yet." She replied that how she felt lately it was as if she was going to die. I held her hand and said we are going to pray and I prayed for her. You could see that it brought her some comfort and she thanked me and said, "I love you, Mike." The evening came and it was time to start our journey back to London. We hugged and kissed and she said she would need me to come back soon to sort some things out. A few weeks past and we phoned each other as normal. She sounded in good spirits.

It was now the start of October 2011 and both my and my aunt's birthday would be the next month, November. She was born on the 14th and I am the 15th, just one day apart. It was the 17th of October and my pastor was visiting me at home. We were just about to leave since I was going to pick up Elizabeth and Joel. As we got outside my house we saw a police car but I did not take much notice. The officer seemed to be looking for someone. He asked, "Are you from number 11?" I said yes, then straight away, Shamar, one of my other sons, came to mind because he had just left the house and he'd had run-ins with the police before so I wondered if it was something with him. Then the officer asked, "Are you Mr Gordon?" I said yes then he said he thought it better if we went inside as he had something to tell me. I said, "What is it? Tell me now," as my auntie's face flashed across my mind. He said, "It is your Aunt." I thought he was going to say she has taken ill and was in hospital. Then he dropped it and said, "She has died." He did not have much information, only that she passed away on the 14th, which was the Friday – three days previously. 'How much more?' I thought. This was my third death in the space of 11 months – yet another funeral to organise. I cannot really describe how I felt at this time.

The next day I had to drive to Bedford to identify the body and register the death. My aunt had given me strict instructions about how she was to be buried. She was yet another one of my loved ones I was going to minister over. Again the horrid question came to mind, WAS SHE SAVED? I have ministered to all of my Family and some close friends concerning the importance of making their peace with the Lord because you cannot do this in the grave.

I know many of you will say how do we know what will happen? First of all, I believe the word of God and it tells us what will happen if we do not accept His Son Jesus Christ as our Lord and Saviour of our life. Think about this: what if I am right? And if I am wrong then it is no problem. But this is my final thought: I am not willing to take the chance, are you?

Chapter 14

IT IS NOT OVER YET

The year 2011 could not have gotten any worse so 2012 has to be better. Well, one thing is evident; Minister Michael Gordon is still alive. God is good. I am constantly wrestling with my illness and now I have an additional problem to deal with. In January, my right side, which was my better side, started to give feelings of numbness, spreading into my right arm, leg, and foot. I know the devil is fuming about me, "This man is a nuisance, encouraging souls to be saved – both young and old; I am going to fix him."

I was driving on a road one day and I went to break, but because of the lack of sensation in my leg, there was no force on the pedal – I could not break and the vehicle was heading full-on into a collision. I realized there was nothing I could do but call on the Lord. If someone had stepped out in front of me they would be dead because I could not stop the vehicle so it would just mow them down. Can you imagine? Knowing that a disaster is going to happen but powerless to stop it? I have never witnessed anything like this in all my 37 years of driving.

But in came the hand of the Lord. I hit a car, full-on in the back, at considerable speed, which could have caused a fatality. When I got out of my car after the initial shock of the impact, I had expected to see the front of my vehicle torn off and the back of the other car with considerable damage. But guess what! There was not one sign of impact apart from the fact that the other car bumper was a fraction out of line! Now listen to this. I told the other driver to let us pull up around the corner so we could exchange details. I got back into my vehicle and you are not going to believe this. My leg went again and I crashed into his car a second time! The startled driver jumped out and asked, "Are you mad?!" I did not blame him; I would have thought the same. Just think. I could have wiped out someone crossing the road, or myself. Consider further that I had just previously come off the motorway, doing 70mph on my way from sorting out my dead aunt's affairs. What if this had happened then?

Writing this book has not been easy for me for many different reasons, but primarily, to replay in my mind all the extreme hurt and turmoil I have been through was daunting. There are numerous other things I could have mentioned herein, but I would never have finished. I therefore decided to stay focused on the greatest Person of all. This book is therefore a tribute to the awesome power of God and the Love of His Son, Jesus Christ my Lord and Saviour, Who shed His blood for the remission of our sins at Calvary. By this I mean to stay true to what I believe with all my heart. Within the extremities of my experiences, joyful moments like the story I shall relate to you now have encouraged my spirit and enabled me to write my book.

My Mother had a brother, my uncle Ronnie, who I knew of but never actually met. My uncle had a daughter, my cousin, called Lona. She visited England in 1976 and spent some time with us. I got on well with her as we had a connection. After her time with us, Lona returned to Jamaica and we kept in touch for a while but then we lost contact. Even when I was living in Jamaica we did not see each other. Just before the death of my aunt in October 2011 (she was the last of three sisters), she and I had spoken about her one and only brother, the father of my cousin Lona. We wondered what had become of him and my cousin.

Now, I had not seen my cousin for thirty-six years and I had never ever seen my uncle. It was my intention to try and find out where my uncle and cousin were, but I did not have a clue where to start. I felt if he was still alive he needed to be informed that his two remaining sisters had passed away. This was going to be almost impossible for me to do but, guess what? For God it was not. A friend of my sister was on holiday in Jamaica and by some incredible divine intervention, he ran into my uncle and told him that we were trying to find him and my cousin. My sister's friend gave my uncle and cousin our telephone numbers and we made contact straight away.

All this happened this year, in May 2012, and we are now reunited and closer than ever. The greatest thing is that all of my Family – my uncle, cousin, cousin's husband and daughter, and her husband, are all Born Again Christians, and now that we have a minister in the Family, well praise God, for we all planned to get together in November when I travel to Jamaica with my Family. We also planned for me to give my testimony at my cousin's church – Edgewater Baptist Church. What a fellowship and reunion that promises to be. Glory be to God.

There are some people who say, "How comes he is serving the Lord and he has not been physically healed yet?" My answer to them is this: the importance is not in the infirmities of my flesh being healed; rather, it is in my spirit and the safe elect of my soul. The body is temporal but the soul is for eternity.

I am not into religion; I am into a relationship with my Lord and Saviour, Jesus Christ. Religion was made up by man and it was the same religious and self righteous that crucified Jesus Christ. Religion is the biggest problem in the world today, which is why my nomination is the Word of God and being led by the Holy Spirit. This Holy Spirit will be restricted in what work He can do within you if all your faith and trust is not exclusively in Jesus Christ and His redemptive work at the Cross. If I were to believe that there are other ways of salvation, such as by works of the flesh, then He died in vain and God would have given His only begotten Son for no reason. The Bible tells us in 1 Corinthians 1:18, "For the preaching of the cross is to them that perish foolishness; but unto us which are saved it is the power of God." Ephesians 2:8-9, "For by grace are ye saved through faith; and that not of yourselves: it is the gift of God: Not of works, lest any man should boast."

Those verses confirm what I am saying; they are not my words, they are the Word of God.

To Him be all Praise and Glory.

SHALL I WRITE A PART TWO? THAT REMAINS TO BE SEEN

Addendum 1 – Sound Warning

There are good sides to the sound system business and also some negative aspects of which I have had more than my share over the years. For example, there are those unscrupulous dance promoters who just completely disrespect a sound man's hard work by trying to avoid paying him. In the earlier days we did not just walk with a record box, we had heavy boxes to lift, from which we often sustained physical injury. Over the years I have played for some of these unscrupulous promoters to whom I have had to show a side of me which I would have preferred not to. One night I and a certain artist ended up kidnapping one promoter, which nearly ended in a fatality.

I was never one to keep malice with another sound man but sometimes one was forced to, because of the behaviour of certain individuals. Nevertheless, when I clashed (competed) with another sound we were enemies during battle, but after that, unless they had a problem, I was cool.

There are many truths that I could reveal but there are enough out there who hate me already so certain things are best left unsaid. Bob Marley said that, "One good thing about music, when it hits you feel no pain." He certainly got that wrong. During my career, I have played certain selections against other sounds and it would have been more bearable for them if I had physically assaulted them.

Over the years I have suffered the loss of many of my valuable tunes, and I am talking about many never-to-be-replaced gems, whether through outright theft or the non-return of borrowed items. When I reflect back on it I have to wonder about the state of some people's conscience.

Let me just finish with this advice. The sound system business is not an easy one if you aim to take it to the professional level. When you are successful, you are really rewarded in every way – with job satisfaction and a sense of giving pleasure to others, with financial reward, a sense of purpose and achievement, and with social acknowledgement and praise. However, on the other hand, I have seen the business wreck personal relationships and lead to mental depression. All of this can come about because of the amount of time and effort required to maintain the business and the disappointment and frustration when expectations fail to manifest. Furthermore, if you love sound system deeply it can turn you into a pauper, causing you to spend your last dime on it. So yes, while sound system can give you both pleasure and heartache, take it from someone like me with lots of experience; if you do not really LOVE sound system do not get involved in it.

Addendum 2 – List of Some Venues and Clashes

These are some of the many venues and areas in the UK and Jamaica that I have played over the years. Some of them you may know:

London venues played

BALI-HI club, Streatham; CLAPHAM MANOR BATHS; EAST DULWICH BATHS; THE SWAN, Stockwell; ROARING TWENTIES CLUB; BRIXTON TOWN HALL; WANDSWORTH TOWN HALL; ACTON TOWN HALL; BROCKWELL PARK; OVAL HOUSE; ACADEMY, Brixton; CAT'S WHISKERS, Streatham; 7-11 GO-GO CLUB, Vauxhall; PODIUM in Vauxhall; ALL NATIONS CLUB, Hackney; GLENGALL, Peckham; BATTERSEA TOWN HALL; GREENWHICH TOWN HALL; CLUB NOREIK, Seven Sisters Road; CUBIES in Dalston; TROJANS, Tottenham; CO-OP HALL, Tooting; LANSDOWNE, Stockwell; ROXY THEATRE, Harlesden; APOLLO CLUB, Willesden; TAVISTOCK in Harlesden; FACTORY (later YAA ASANTEWAA), Chippenham Mews; TELEGRAPH, Brixton Hill; SHEPHERD'S, Railton Road; NORWOOD LIBRARY; NORWOOD HALL; ACTION CENTRE in Waterloo; KING ON THE RYE, Peckham; DICK SHEPHERD, Tulse Hill; ALBANY INSTITUTE, Creek Rd, Deptford; ABENG (later KARIBU), Brixton; MR.BEES/BOUNCING BALL, Peckham; DEPTFORD CRYPT; MOONSHOT, New Cross; CLOUDS, Brixton Road; BALHAM 200; BURTON'S in Cricklewood; ST GILES, Camberwell; PEOPLE'S CLUB (formerly Count Suckle's Q Club), Paddington; and ACKLAM HALL, Acklam Road, Ladbroke Grove.

UK Country venues played

NEWLANDS CLUB, High Wycombe; MFM, Sheep St in Northampton, CLEOPATRA, Huddersfield; DIGBETH CIVIC HALL, Birmingham; MOSS SIDE CENTRE, Manchester; MARCUS GARVEY CENTRE, Bristol; and other venues in Leeds, Bradford, Coventry, Bedford, Luton, Derby, Reading, Wolverhampton, Walsall, Milton Keynes, Nottingham, Sheffield, Leicester, Oxford, Blackpool, Gloucester, Ipswich, and Norwich.

Jamaica Venues/Areas played

STAND PIPE, Kingston; SKATELAND, Half Way Tree; HOUSE OF LEO Cargill Avenue, Half Way Tree; MAMA IVY'S in August Town; CHISHOLM AVENUE, Kingston; TAURUS CLUB, Royal Flat, Manchester; WINNERS, Waltham Park Road, Kingston; ASCOT DRIVE IN, Old Harbour; JACK RUBY LAWN, James Avenue in Ocho Rios; as well as other venues in Mandeville, Porus and Christiana in Manchester; May Pen and Spalding in Clarendon; St. Elizabeth, Trelawny, St. Ann, St Mary, Kingston; St. Andrew; Blue Mountain; Portland; Spanish Town, Old Harbour and Portmore in St. Catherine; Negril in Westmoreland; and Montego Bay in St. James.

These are some of the sounds I have clashed (competed) with over the years:

London Sounds clashed with

SIR COXSONE; SAXON; JAH SHAKA; MOA AMBASSA; KING TUBBY'S; JAH TUBBYS; FRONTLINE; JAVA; LORD KOOS; SMALL AXE; FATMAN; LORD GELLY'S; COUNT SHELLY; D-NUNES; YOUNG LION; NEGAS NUGAS; LORD DAVID; UNITY; I SPY; SUPERTONE; EXODUS; and HAWKEYE.

UK Country Sounds clashed with

QUAKER CITY, Birmingham; JUNGLE MAN, Birmingham; and MAFIATONE, Birmingham.

Jamaican Sounds clashed with

JAH WORKS, Mandeville, Manchester; RAY SYMBOLIC, Kingston; COSMIC FORCE, Clarendon; BLACK ZODIAC, Kingston; BLACKSTAR, Kingston; BLACK LION, St. Mary; GT INTERNATIONAL, Kingston; CREATION ROCK TOWER, Spanish Town, YOUTH PROMOTION (Sugar Minott's Sound), Robert Crescent, Kingston; SOUL TREE, Christiana, Manchester; BLACK ORGAN, St. Elizabeth; KANGOL, St. Ann; INNER CITY, Kingston; and CONCORD, Clarendon.

Lightning Source UK Ltd.
Milton Keynes UK
UKOW031154220213

206665UK00005B/97/P